CURRICULUM ISSUES IN ARTS EDUCATION VOLUME 2

THE
AESTHETIC IMPERATIVE
Relevance and Responsibility
in Arts Education

CURRICULUM ISSUES IN ARTS EDUCATION

Series Editor: Malcolm Ross, University of Exeter

Vol. 1. The Arts and Personal Growth

Vol. 2. The Aesthetic Imperative

Vol. 3. The Development of Aesthetic Experience

A related Pergamon journal *

EVALUATION IN EDUCATION

Editors: B. H. Choppin and T. N. Postlethwaite

The aim of this series is to inform those involved in educational evaluation in both developing and developed countries of progress in the various aspects of the theory and practice in educational evaluation.

* Free specimen copies available on request

THE
AESTHETIC IMPERATIVE
Relevance and Responsibility
in Arts Education

Edited by

MALCOLM ROSS
University of Exeter

PERGAMON PRESS
OXFORD · NEW YORK · TORONTO · SYDNEY · PARIS · FRANKFURT

U.K.	Pergamon Press Ltd., Headington Hill Hall, Oxford OX3 OBW, England
U.S.A.	Pergamon Press Inc., Maxwell House, Fairview Park, Elmsford, New York 10523, U.S.A.
CANADA	Pergamon Press Canada Ltd., Suite 104, 150 Consumers Rd., Willowdale, Ontario M2J 1P9, Canada
AUSTRALIA	Pergamon Press (Aust.) Pty. Ltd., P.O. Box 544, Potts Point, N.S.W. 2011, Australia
FRANCE	Pergamon Press SARL, 24 rue des Ecoles, 75240 Paris, Cedex 05, France
FEDERAL REPUBLIC OF GERMANY	Pergamon Press GmbH, 6242 Kronberg-Taunus, Hammerweg 6, Federal Republic of Germany

First edition 1981
Reprinted 1982

British Library Cataloguing in Publication Data

The Aesthetic imperative. -(Curriculum issues in
arts education; V.2)
1. Educational accountability - Great Britain
2. Art teachers - Great Britain
I. Ross, Malcolm
379.1'5   LB2806
ISBN 0-08-026766-1

Library of Congress Catalog Card No. 81-82524

In order to make this volume available as economic-
ally and as rapidly as possible the author's typescript
has been reproduced in its original form. This method
unfortunately has its typographical limitations but it is
hoped that they in no way distract the reader.

Printed in Great Britain by A Wheaton & Co. Ltd., Exeter

Introduction to the Series

MALCOLM ROSS

This series of books springs from a particular
impulse: a feeling that those of us active in the
field of arts education must redouble our efforts to
ensure the greater effectiveness of our work.

The impulse is strong, the felt need a matter of
urgency, even emergency. It arose against a background of economic cuts-back and ideological reactiv-
ism: the troubles besetting our society were being
identified not merely by the politicians and econo-
mists but by the populace in general with the alleged
failure of the schools to produce suitably trained
personnel for the country's industrial and techno-
logical needs. With the judgment that we'd all been
having it too good (and on the cheap). And with the
call to apply the strictest, most utilitarian and
cost-effective criteria to an overall assessment of
our society, the way it works, the services it relies
upon and the output it generates. In such a climate
we should expect the arts, arts education, the life
of feeling, intuitive knowing and the things of the
spirit all to be severely tested - and, as I write,
the evidence offers all too plain an endorsement.

But I should like to think that we might have launched
this project even in less searching times - for the
impulse is not merely a reflex act in self defence as
it were. Behind the decision regularly to publish a
collection of papers treating the arts in education
not as separate subjects but as a <u>single discipline</u>
lies the conviction that it is only through the
recognition of their common educational function (as
distinct from their separate several identities and

processes) that the arts will ever come to play the significant part in the education of everyone, young or old, artistically gifted or otherwise, that we confidently proclaim they should. It is because we feel that arts teachers, artists and everyone involved in arts education wherever and at whatever level they work must find common cause, discover their common interest and express themselves as far as possible in a common language, that this series has been conceived. Our hope is that these books – and the conferences from which, in large measure, they will derive – will make a useful contribution to the establishing of this sense of identity and towards the strengthening of the hands of individual teachers in their efforts to create the appropriate grounds for their encounters with those whose feeling lives they seek to enliven and enhance.

The following topics will be the subject of further issues and conferences:

1. Arts Education and Aesthetic Development
2. Arts Education and Contemporary Arts
3. The Core of the Arts Curriculum.

Preface

In the Preface to the preceding volume in this series
I promised that the theme of Assessment in the Arts
would feature strongly in the present one - and a
glance at the contents page will show that I have
kept my word. But this year's papers are not concerned only with the assessment issue. We have, in
fact, tried to set that particular question in a
wider context: that of the relevance of the arts in
the curriculum as a whole, and of the special responsibilities that fall upon arts teachers by virtue of
the subjects they teach. Since the publication of
the last volume the D.E.S. has made a good deal
clearer its curricular intentions - in particular we
now know much more about the so-called "core curriculum". In view of the implicit threat against the
arts subjects that these pronouncements contain it
seemed important to concentrate our efforts this year
upon the central issue of accountability. So I have
invited contributions from a group of distinguished
educators on different aspects of this topic, ranging
from on the one hand an assessment of the whole system of public examinations, especially as applied to
the arts, and on the other to an account of arts education that stresses the development of the sense of
personal worth. Clearly arts teachers must be able
both to give a good account of themselves and to
offer hard and acceptable evidence of the educational
value of what they do.

The bulk of the papers in the present volume were delivered at the University of Exeter's Creative Arts
Summer School, held at Dillington House College from
the 26th July until the 2nd August 1980. The theme
of the conference was "Relevance and Responsibility
in Arts Education" and my own paper "Hard Core: the
Dilemma of the Arts" (originally published in Exeter

University's Perspectives 2:   The Core Curriculum)
was used as the baseline for the papers, debates and
activities that followed. Professor Louis Arnaud
Reid was asked particularly to consider the philosophical aspects of the assessment question and it
was interesting and illuminating to have his qualified endorsement of the idea of national monitoring.
This topic generated on the whole both heat and light
in equal proportions with few participants taking up
extreme positions. But interest was fervent, as the
following extract from a post-conference letter indicates. It comes from Christopher Beedell of Bristol
University. I quote it because it expresses very
well the feeling shared by many participants at the
conference that whereas assessment between pupil and
teacher, joint participants in the educational encounter, was entirely acceptable and indeed wholly
necessary, developments such as the APU constituted a
considerable threat to the quality and integrity of
arts education.

> "I think the guts of my position is that
> artistic expression - whether it takes
> the form of a deep ritual affirmation of
> a view of a part of the world, or con-
> trarily affirms a personal feeling and
> understanding of a part of the world in
> a way which is contrary to the received
> perception - is basically a collective
> enterprise. I think that collective is
> made up of the maker, those from whom
> the maker has learnt and the maker's
> audience. It is that 'constituency'
> which the maker trusts in order to have
> the courage to undertake the making, and
> it is that constituency which the maker
> trusts to evaluate what is made. In
> school, the makers, teachers and peers
> are the living and present part of the
> collective. The local parents and com-
> munity should also be part of that
> collective, but rarely are. What is
> 'manipulative' and false to the process
> of making is the attempt to represent
> the collective by replacing it with ex-
> ternal assessors. To do that is to

"gobble up the meaning of the made. A
process which is truer to the making
and the trust it assumes in <u>shared</u>
power could involve 'arbiters' but only
insofar as their judgment was set
alongside and shared with that of the
maker's constituency. This implies a
'convivial' form of assessment which
is, I suspect, far from anything that
would satisfy the DES."

It is most valuable to be able to include two substantial statements on this general theme, both successful I think in shedding helpful light upon a
highly complex and controversial issue. I refer to
the papers by Professor David Aspin and Ernest Goodman. Both Mr Goodman and myself are members of the
APU working party on "Aesthetic Development": my
own lecture on the APU's work has not been included
here on the grounds that it might be felt to break
confidentiality.

The conference made progress I think in straightening
out some of the confusion that often seems to attend
the discussion of assessment in the arts by recognising that we need to distinguish between the quite
different purposes - and therefore the necessarily
different procedures - of national monitoring, of
national public examinations, of LEA assessment of
schools and of in-school assessment of children's
artistic and aesthetic development. At the most
basic level we saw an important difference of focus
between what teachers sought to know about the progress of their own pupils (knowing them by their
fruits as it were) and what a programme of national
monitoring might seek to disclose (knowing that general performance levels were stable, rising or falling). Though there were strong voices raised against
certain features and forms of assessment - instanced,
for example, in the papers by Ben Bradnack and Professor Harry Reé - there seemed to be general unanim-
ity that it was a vitally important and urgent matter
to achieve effective and appropriate forms of assessment in arts education.

The last three papers in this volume rather draw

away from assessment to consider more general though
related matters. Peter Abbs makes an authoritative
case for the re-ordering of English studies within
the general field of the expressive arts and his
analysis of the changes of emphasis in English teaching over the last fifty years or so suggests interesting parallels among the other, more traditional
arts subjects. I for one would like to see what he
asks of English teachers generally accepted among
music, art and drama teachers. Victor Heyfron spoke
towards the end of the conference about the notion of
relevance and his argument for a position midway between the extreme of "instrumentality" and "self-
sufficiency" (not a term he uses) I find both per-
suasive and welcome. He manages to say, clearly and
reasonably, some of the more important things that I
am only feeling my way toward in my own, concluding,
essay.

I believe it to be imperative for the arts to assert
their crucial role in a balanced and humane curriculum. It is equally imperative for arts teachers to
supply both the arguments and the evidence needed if
their work is to survive and, indeed, develop significantly. We hope this volume and the conference
from which it is principally derived will have made a
useful contribution to the cause we care about so
much. In conclusion I would once again like to thank
the Michael Marks Charitable Trust for continuing
invaluable support, without which the work of the
Arts Curriculum Project at Exeter University would
not be possible. Thanks also, as always, to Peter
Epps and his colleagues at Dillington House, and my
own colleagues whose efforts made the Summer School
of 1980 particularly successful.

Malcolm Ross

Contents

xii

Contents

Contributors

PETER ABBS,   Lecturer in Education, University of
   Sussex.

DAVID ASPIN, Professor of Education, Kings College,
   London University.

BEN BRADNACK, Head of Drama, Itchen College,
   Southampton.

ERNEST GOODMAN, MBE., formerly Headmaster,
   Manchester High School of Art. Chairman, The
   Schools Council Art Panel.

VICTOR HEYFRON,   Principal Lecturer, Worcester
   College of Higher Education.

HARRY RÉE, formerly Professor of Education at York
   University.

LOUIS ARNAUD REID, Professor Emeritus of Philosophy
   of Education, University of London Institute of
   Education.

MALCOLM ROSS, Lecturer in Arts Education and
   Director of the Arts Curriculum Project at Exeter
   University School of Education.

The typescript was prepared by Mary Bellamy

Hard Core:
The Predicament of the Arts
MALCOLM ROSS

"We are experiencing not the destruction
of every whole, every unit or unity,
every meaning, but rather the rule and
power of the whole, the super-imposed,
administered unification. Not disin-
tegration but the reproduction and
integration of that which is, is the
catastrophe." (Herbert Marcuse, 1979)

A Framework for the Curriculum (1980) - hereafter referred to as Framework is, on the face of it, bad news
for the arts. With the curious exception of literature the arts don't figure among the subjects reserved to the core of the curriculum. Although the
words 'aesthetic' and 'creative' appear on page 3 as,
together, constituting one of eight areas of experience with which the curriculum should be concerned,
the reader has to wait until the last page (paragraph
32) for the subjects usually thought of as 'the arts'
to receive a specific mention. The section that includes the arts (along with craft, design, technology,
history, geography, careers, moral and health education, etc. etc.) is headed "Preparation for adult and
working life" - from which one draws certain conclusions about their perceived educational function.
Schools, so the document observes, will be under in-
tense pressure and the non-core subjects will have to
be fitted in as best as possible, perhaps as special
topics taught as short courses, perhaps allowed some
scope within the teaching of the core subjects. However - indeed whether - the arts figure, their lowly
status is made perfectly clear.

1

The banishment of the arts, is now, apparently, to be
officially sanctioned. This is not an unremarkable
event for, despite the frequent actual neglect of the
arts in education, almost every official pronouncement has hitherto argued for the recognition of their
uniquely important educational role. Newsom (1963),
for instance, recognised that the arts subjects
"offer creative and civilising influences beneficial
to all pupils". Lord Goodman, speaking in the House
of Lords on the 19th April 1967, declared his faith
in the educational impact of the arts upon the
young: "Once young people are captured for the arts
they are redeemed from many of the dangers which confront them". Whether you share his faith or not it
is the kind of claim that a great many arts teachers
have traditionally made. One wonders whether such
sentiments would be even possible from such a quarter
today.

Times have indeed changed. There is almost no way of
bridging the gulf that now divides us from the 60s.
The Western world has suffered a series of economic
and moral disasters: the promise of those days has
proved irredeemable. And we are facing a growing
number of seemingly insoluble problems: spiralling
inflation and unemployment, failing industry, increased lawlessness, robot take-over and the return
of the threat of nuclear war. All this against a
background of apparent political bankruptcy. Yeats'
vision of the Second Coming, the sense of things
falling apart, the fear that the centre cannot hold,
seems awesomely immanent. In such circumstances it is
perhaps not surprising that we should see, at Govern-
ment level, a desperate attempt to superimpose, in
Marcuse's words, an "administered unification". The
disarmingly simple argument of Framework that says
we must decide upon the basic education the country
needs and then ordain it is but one instance of the
advancing 'rule and power of the whole'. Which is
not to say that arts teachers do not have to provide
their own answers to the crisis we are all facing.
Few would argue with the assessment that the whole
area of public expenditure needs to be critically examined and priorities decided upon. Within the educational field such a view of aims and practices is
entirely unexceptionable - indeed the argument for a

balanced educational experience for all children that
would develop their minds, bodies and spirits while
at the same time taking into account the interests
and needs of the country is just plain sense. We
surely must think about these things. What matters
is the quality of that thinking, which is where
Framework fails so grossly. And it is upon the quality of that thinking that I wish to concentrate in
this paper. The propriety of the encroachments of
the D.E.S. upon the professional responsibilities of
teachers is discussed elsewhere. (Perspectives 2,1980).

Nowhere is the idea of balance specifically examined.
That is to say there is no analysis of the terms in
which the curricular elements are weighed against
each other, set in some kind of appositional or com-
plimentary relationship. The composition of the core
discloses a severely restricted account of the growth
of the human mind. The truth of the package is somehow or other supposed to be self-evident. The inden-
tification of the elements to be so balanced with the
traditional school subjects compounds the dubious
nature of the paper's conclusions. A serious review
of the school curriculum, prompted by questions of
efficiency and relevance, must begin with a radical
appraisal of the concept of curriculum itself. We
might, for instance, question the continued usefulness of the division of the curriculum into traditional subjects. There are alternatives after all, such
as the holistic model (the idea of the 'whole'
curriculum) or the 'lines of development' under-
pinning the work of the APU. We need to ask ourselves
what kind of a balance we are trying to strike before
looking at the particular ways in which children's
experience is to be modified and structured. I have
myself argued elsewhere for a three dimensional model
of the curriculum that distinguishes fields of knowledge (subject constellations), ways of knowing (expressive and impressive - see Witkin, 1974), and
media of representation (enactive, iconic and symbolic - see Bruner, 1978).

> "The principle of my Whole Curriculum
> is that key concepts would be identi-
> fied and worked as projects drawing the
> various subject disciplines together

> and ensuring a full, rounded response
> to the expressive and impressive aspects
> of human experience. The key concepts
> (the problems to be projected) would be
> decided by the teaching staff as a whole
> and the particularity of the curriculum
> for specific groups of children worked
> out by the teams of teachers responsible
> for their learning." (Ross, 1978)

I proposed five fields of knowledge (there are other
ways of integrating subjects about a central knowledge concept): Language, Maths and Science, Creative
Arts, Humanitites and Religion, Technology. Such an
approach embodies a specific view of human experience
and of the way we learn and grow - an holistic view.
I would argue that such a view has much to offer in
meeting the needs of the foreseeable future. It derives from some kind of an assessment of what that
future, given there is to be one, would be like. If
there happened to be schools somewhere prepared to
give this idea a try it would be nice to think that
they were free to do so.

I do not suggest in my model that any decisions about
the curriculum need to be or ever should be taken
other than at local level. That is because I prefer
the judgment of those most immediately involved in
the educational encounter to any remote, administra-
tive edict-making. It depends of course how you
conceive of change and development in any field of
experience. Rather than legislating to "reproduce
and integrate that which is" I prefer to allow
changes to evolve, to monitor them as they occur,
and generally see that the system as a whole is
aware, responsive and behaving responsibly. The ways
a people grows, a culture unfolds, are largely in-
scrutable. I am fairly confident that cultural development resists edicts and "administered uniform-
ity". It has to do so because the basic law of evolution is differentiation, variety, flexibility. We
are more likely to achieve a suitable curriculum for
the next twenty years by encouraging diversity, by
funding local initiatives and by monitoring the responses of informed and committed individuals than by
a policy of centralised unification that cynically

usurps the basic expertise and duties of the professional teacher. What is wrong with Framework is its
completely trivial perception of the nature of the
issues it purports to deal with. Of course the real
educational debate hasn't yet begun, indeed may never
begin.

This is not the place to rehearse at length the case
for a major educational function for the arts but it
might, nevertheless, be useful to reflect upon some
of the possible ways in which the arts could respond
to the sentence apparently to be passed upon them.
I have already said that the obligation to explain,
share and render an account of praxis is as incumbent
upon a teacher of the arts as upon anyone else, despite the not inconsiderable difficulties of doing so.
(No one for instance in this field yet speaks with
absolute confidence on either art or aesthetics!) I
fear there may be some teachers who will choose to
meet the challenge on its own terms ie. defend the
value of what they are doing on the grounds of practical utility. They might argue for instance that
art gives to-morrow's designers a sharper eye and a
creative turn of mind; that drama produces young
people with presence, the kind of self-confidence
that impresses employers, and a sensitivity to social
and inter-personal problems; that music is a civil-
ized way of letting off steam and, like drama, en-
courages group co-operation and sensitivity to others.

They will probably also be happy to go along with
those who see future unemployment as an occasion for
increased leisure. Who better, the argument runs,
than the arts people to prepare us for all that spare
time? The concept of leisure, however, is the inven-
tion of those who equate work with supervised
drudgery.

Hopefully the electronic revolution will make such
drudgery less prevalent and free people, not to be-
have as the leisurely unemployed but to take a greater
hand in determining and regulating their own working
lives.   I have always been in the privileged position of being paid to do work that was its own reward and to continue my own education through life.
I do not think it unreasonable to suppose that this

kind of opportunity might become more and more generally available. I can see no inherent reason why we
shouldn't welcome the opportunities that are coming
nor why anyone will have needed an arts education
specifically geared to fitting them out for a future
of mental weightlessness. This points, I think, to
the flaw in thinking about the arts in terms of the
labour - leisure dialectic. The case for the arts
must rest not upon their worldliness but upon their
other-worldliness, not upon their usefulness but upon
their uselessness, not upon their promise of consolation but upon the revolutionary vision of a better
life.

In his recent book, The Aesthetic Dimension Marcuse
insists that art speaks to revolutionary practice
from another world. It is the business of art he
says to re-work reality, to 'explode' the myth that
everyday existence is somehow truer than the world
the artist creates in answer to the needs of his
feelings, passion and imagination. Marcuse sees art
as nurturing, consistently and continuously, by its
very nature, the revolutionary, creative instinct -
what he calls "the struggle for the impossible against
the unconquerable".

The predicament of the arts in education may be no
worse today than it has ever been. For one thing
recent years have seen a marked improvement in the
willingness and ability of arts educators to argue
their case; the worm has already turned and is giving
a good account of itself. I am sure the arts have
never been better taught nor had a stronger following
among young people, both in and outside school. And,
despite the apparent drift towards materialistic
self-interest, there are signs everywhere that people
recognise there is an important dimension missing
from their lives: the aesthetic dimension, the dimension of quality. These are not, of course, times
for complacency, but neither should we be too des-
pondent. Framework, one guesses, is not simply bad
news for the arts, it is bad news for education. In
the outraged response it ought to evoke the arts will
not, I think, be the only voices of dissent.

REFERENCES

Bruner, Jerome S. (1978) Towards a Theory of
    Instruction, Harvard University Press.

Department of Education and Science. (1980) A
    Framework for the Curriculum. H.M.S.O.

Marcuse, Herbert. (1979) The Aesthetic Dimension.
    Macmillan Press Ltd.

Ross, Malcolm. (1978) The Creative Arts. Heinemann
    Educational Books.

Witkin, R.W. (1974) The Intelligence of Feeling.
    Heinemann Educational Books.

Assessment and Aesthetic Education

LOUIS ARNAUD REID

This paper was written, and delivered as a lecture,
at a time (mid-summer 1980) when the work for the
arts section of the Assessment of Performance Unit
was in a transitional stage. I have not been a member of the committee concerned with this, but I have
had the privilege of knowing two people who have been
members. I have seen some earlier tentative drafts
of proposals, and have discussed them very fully,
over two years, with four groups of my advanced students (all artists of one kind or another and teachers or lecturers in the arts). What I have to say
here has been much influenced by these glimpses and
discussions - though I am now speaking for myself
alone. I shall not be discussing directly the work
of the (Arts) A.P.U., but I shall, at the end of the
paper, briefly allude to some of the fears and misgivings to which the very existence of 'monitoring'
the arts has given rise.

We are concerned here with broad questions of the
nature of art education in schools and particularly
how, or maybe whether, it should be assessed. I
think that in order even to begin to consider these
questions we have first to look back at our general
ideas of what the arts and the aesthetic really are.
It does not of course follow that all that we think
about the aesthetic and art can be transferred
directly into school life. There are in fact always
particular and empirical considerations, and infinitely varied classroom situations, which have to be
taken into practical account before any general
theories can be 'applied' to practice. Nevertheless
without as clear general concepts as we can get,

8

practical policies are apt to be confused, direction-
less.   There are here involved two distinguishable
but related questions: What is art and the aesthetic?
What should we do about them in schools?

Take the <u>aesthetic</u> first, as it is in some ways a
broader concept than art.   There are two aspects of
the aesthetic, subjective and objective, the
aesthetic attitude, and the object of the attitude.
The aesthetic attitude is exemplified whenever we attend to, enjoy contemplatively, anything 'for its own
sake', for itself, for its intrinsic interestingness
- and not for the sake of increasing factual or conceptual knowledge, or for practical or any other external reasons.   The object, for its part, must be
sufficiently interesting to hold our attention.   The
object can be anything whatever, provided it is
sufficiently interesting to hold the attention.   Patterns of abstract ideas - e.g. mathematics - can be
aesthetic 'objects'; but here we shall be thinking
mainly of visual and perhaps auditory perceptions - of
colours, sounds, patterns of them, textures, forms of
all kinds.   These are, of course, included in the
qualities of art, but aesthetic interest extends far
beyond art to the whole realm of nature and to human
constructs which are not as such art.

The <u>work of art</u>, from the artist's point of view, is
something made with aesthetic intention (whether fully
conscious intention or not), something that can be
contemplated and enjoyed for its own sake, and also
something which expresses and embodies in a perceived
material medium values, ideas, meanings, which could
not possibly be expressed and embodied - and so known
- in any other way.   Through his active transaction,
or intercourse, with the material medium, the artist
is able to discover, to come to know, to feel, in
perceiving the object he has made, a kind of intrinsic
untranslatable significance which only art can give.
This is true of any art - of visual arts like sculpture, painting, of poetry, drama, music - though of
course the meanings are of very different kinds, pe-
culiar to each art.   You can say things in poetry
which can't be said in prose;   in drama which can't
be said in music, in music what can only be 'said'
uniquely there.   The artist does not just 'express

himself', or express the thoughts or feelings which were in his mind before he made the art. To think this is the commonest of mistakes not only popularly but even among some sophisticated aestheticians. It is important to recognise that always art for the artist is discovery of what was not there before. It is so for us too, the receivers of art. Something new is presented in the embodiment we perceive. It has individual, concrete character which has to be attended to, studied in a way which often involves mental activities of different kinds, and, if the work is worth it, the study may take a long time.

Of aesthetic education outside the arts I will not say much; it is not in the centre of the 'assessment' problem. But this does not mean that it is not very important. Parents' and teachers' encouragement of children in the enjoyment of natural beauty, for instance, can open their eyes - and indeed stimulate all their senses - to what they might not otherwise be aware of, though unspoiled children, I think, have a basic natural openness to such things. The sense of the ambience of the natural world - sky, light, clouds, sea, distant horizons, the air breathed deeply, the support and smells of the earth and growing things ... - this can be a constant and unending source of joy, perhaps in a way an archetypal kind of joy. So too of the physically smaller aspects of nature - forms, textures, colours of trees, flowers, fruits, animals large or small ... - 'found' objects of every kind. Attention to any and all of these (and much more), simply for what they are, is aesthetic attention, intrinsically good in itself, as well as instrumentally good as a basis and preparation for the more or less sophisticated constructions of art. This last point can be significant. A recurring question comes from uninitiates into more abstract visual arts: 'What does it mean? (It occurs sometimes in relation to music too.) 'Meaning' here has the suggestion of 'referential' meaning. But if the texture of a moss-grown stone or the shape of a shell or the glory of a mountain range can be enjoyed for their own sakes, without questions of 'What does it mean?' being raised, why not - at least in the first instance - a presented piece of art? Art 'says' its meaning directly: it cannot ever be said adequately

in words that are other than part of an art (in
poetry, for instance).

Another field of interest, and important for
aesthetic education, is the 'built environment' and
whole areas of design and craft. These are areas of
the man-made, with important aesthetic aspects, sometimes, but not necessarily, coming within the desig-
nation of 'works of art'. It is debatable whether
some churches, public buildings, country mansions,
gardens, whole areas like Hampstead Garden Suburb,
can unambiguously be called 'works of art'. The same
applies to the shapes of motor cars, fridges, kitchen
and tableware, furniture ... But whatever they are
called, the encouragement of enlightened attention to
them has great significance for both personal and social life.

But our concern here is with 'art' - and here mainly
the visual arts.

Art is a human making, 'with aesthetic intention';
and it is also a made thing, to be contemplated and
enjoyed. The notable artists of history or of recent
contemporary life have been distinguished men whose
art (for the most part) has been their life work.
Children, or the adolescents whom I have mainly in
mind here, are not distinguished artists, or are not
yet so; and most of the run of the mill are (by definition) not highly talented. On the other hand one
of the things which all artists do is to work in some
medium and to discover meaning in and through it.
Working in some medium is something all children can
learn something from. Working in a medium in itself
can be fascinating, sometimes revealing, sometimes
new-life-giving experience, whether it is oil or
acrylic paint, or guache, or clay, or wood or stone.
It can also help towards the understanding of artists
who work in these media. It is only a beginning, of
course, and necessarily limited in its scope. Perhaps it is platitudinous to say this; yet it is
necessary, since 'messing about' in a medium is sometimes about all that 'art education' amounts to.
Messing about has to be at least purposive - and it
is the kind of exploratory purposiveness which art-
making is, that all have to learn. This too is only

a beginning. It is a trying to make, imaginatively,
coherent constructions out of media - pots, figures;
carvings, sculptures; pictures, collages... Here
talent (or the limitations of talent) will show more.
But the experience itself, for those who enter into
it willingly, or at least co-operatively, can be a
rewarding discovery of embodied meaning which could
not be known in any other way. I do not need to say
how much good art departments in schools have contributed to the offering of varied opportunities for
the initiation into the initiation of experience in
art making. The fact that sometimes exaggerated
claims have been made, or that too much has been
made of 'self-expression' (rather than the discovery
of new values in embodiment which are other than
'oneself', and are part of a continuing process of
discovery) - this does nothing to lessen the importance of the educational value of the real thing.

Some exceptional pupils require special attentions -
of so many kinds that I shall not attempt to start
exemplifying them. Perhaps a very few indeed will
become professional artists. The school teacher's
job is certainly not to make them into that (and of
course no teacher can 'make' an artist), but to
give them the help they specifically need as and when
they require it.

What of the rest, who have had, let us suppose, the
opportunities for art making but who have not been
able to achieve much? Are they, from now on, to be
dropped from 'art education'? After all, what is
'art education'? Some of it is as we have described.
But there is another, and in one sense a much wider
aspect of art education - and one which is certainly
not for the less talented performers only, but for
every single pupil. I mean the skillful initiation
into learning to look (listen, etc.) with discriminating attention, critical enjoyment and appraisal at
given works of art. And if it be true that art departments on the whole have catered well for the
practical side of art making, it seems equally true
to me, from all I hear from many advanced students
who as art teachers have been through art schools
and teacher training, that what Harry Broudy has so
appropriately called 'enlightened cherishing', has

been quite shamefully neglected. There is what
Harold Osborne in his turn has called the 'art' of
appreciation. In <u>this</u> art, art teachers seem to have
had little or no education. Teachers of course show
their pupils works of art and take them from time to
time to galleries and museums - a great opportunity
for their further education. But, as I have frequently heard it said, teachers simply 'do not know
what to say' to the children. It is not necessarily
their fault if indeed they have had no training in
critical methods. (Contrast the fully trained teacher
of English, who has been steeped in it.) It is more
than high time that art schools and training institutions for art teachers in this country were given at
least a systematic introduction to visual art criticism.

This would be a good thing in itself; but if we are
thinking of schools, it is the teacher's ability to
teach criticism in the classroom which is important.
By 'criticism' here I mean discriminating appraisal
of given works of art; I do not of course identify
criticism with fault-finding - though it may include
that.

Criticism in the classroom is of course far too complex a theme to be fully elucidated or discussed here.
I shall therefore only refer to an excellent article
on the subject by Ralph A. Smith in the <u>Journal of
Aesthetic Education</u> (Vol. 7, No. 1, January, 1973).
Smith distinguishes two broad facets of criticism,
the Exploratory and the Evaluative. They overlap and
cannot be separated from one another. There are no
hard and fast rules of criticism. But the Exploratory aspect can be divided into three stages - Description, Characterisation and Analysis, Interpretation. 'Description' is pretty matter of fact -
identifying and naming the major components of a work,
such as subject matter and formal structures. It
might include putting a work into its historical
context. The first main function of description is
to get people to attend, notice, reflect, make a
preliminary analysis. 'Characterisation and Analysis' is a development of the same kind of thing, but
perhaps attending more closely to the ways in which
the elements of the description dispose themselves

into a variety of forms and patterns. It is impossible to dissociate this from some measure of evaluation, if only in the greater emphasis on <u>what</u> to
notice. We interpret as we see. On the other hand
the act of 'interpretation' is <u>logically</u> distinct
from description or evaluation. 'Interpretation' is
the apprehension of overall meaning, the sort of
import which emerges from what Smith calls the
"interanimation of materials, subject matter, and
form". 'Evaluation' which includes aesthetic 'argument') is the fruit of what has gone before, an
emergent from it. Smith sums it up well. "If
asked to justify his evaluation a responsible critic
ought to be able to argue in favor of his assessment. This he can do by <u>re</u>describing, <u>re</u>analysing,
and so on, what he has already noticed for himself.
He thus attempts in aesthetic argument to persuade
others that the object is in fact reasonably seen,
heard, or taken in the way his interpretation and
judgment have stated. He may do all of this with
quite an armament of verbal and nonverbal critical
techniques. Indeed, the resources a critic can use
are practically limitless. He may...point out again
both nonaesthetic and aesthetic features and how
they are linked; or he may vivify with simile and
metaphor, compare and contrast, reiterate and varie-
gate, and so on. Nonverbally, he may draw on a
repertoire of bodily gestures and facial expressions,
which can also be effective tools of persuasion".
Two points stand out; that critical evaluation
comes logically last, and that the aim of the whole
process is to get other people to see and feel, and
if possible <u>enjoy for themselves</u>, and with discrimination, what is before them. It can be an initiation
of a lifelong joy.

So far I have mentioned several items in the complex
of aesthetic education: aesthetic response and enjoyment - to anything perceived and enjoyed and contemplated for itself, whether natural things, or
things made by man, art or not. This can include
enjoyment of working in the media of art. Then there
is the essaying to make works of art themselves,
more or less successfully. And there is the learning to be discriminatingly, critically appreciative.
Can these things be assessed? Should they be? If

so, how?

Aesthetic sensitivity and responsiveness is a condition of anything which can be called 'art' happening at all. It is like the 'charity' or love mentioned in the New Testament, without which everything
else is worthless. You can have the best will in the
world, knowledge <u>about</u> nature and art, the best
technical skills: it is of no avail without aesthetic sensitivity. If this is true, as it is, one might
be moved to say at once that this is, above everything else, the most important thing to be tested
and assessed. But one would be wrong; partly because responsiveness cannot adequately be tested,
and partly because even if it could be - and in some
degree perhaps it can - it is not the sort of thing
which ought to be 'assessed'. By 'assessed' here I
mean marked up or down on some scale, or measured,
perhaps competitively, against others. Of course
sensitive response can to some extent be shown 'pub-
licly' to others - to a teacher for instance - by
behaviour or perhaps speech. We can 'see' a person's delight in a shell or a leaf or a piece of
art, or hear his expressions of joy. But sensitive
response is in the first and last instance a personal
and private thing, known fully only by the person
experiencing it. The fact that it can up to a point
be expressed in action or speech is no contradiction
of its primal privacy. To be enchanted, charmed,
moved by the qualities of this particular and individual thing in this particular way is something the
person himself alone can know intuitively and directly. And this in itself not only cannot be 'assessed'
by anyone else: it is not the sort of thing that
ought to be 'assessed' even if, per <u>impossibile</u>, it
could. It is a gift from heaven rather than a human
achievement to be put on a comparative scale.

But the fact that this priceless gift cannot, and
should not <u>in and by itself</u> be assessed, in no way
implies that its essential presence within every
single experience of the aesthetic in art or outside
it cannot be manifested or shown both in the making
of art, the made art, and in the appraisal of given
works of art. One can watch a sensitive painter
painting, and <u>see</u> (with some aesthetic insight) in

the immediate expressiveness of his painting movements - a bit of this colour here, a balancing
stroke there, the unifying sweep of a rhythmic ges-
ture - his artistic sensitivity. The spectator is
not the painter, who has his own private experiences and impulses which the spectator cannot directly
know. The spectator is not 'seeing' those private
ongoings; but the relation between the mind and body
in art, and the relation of the mind and body to the
movement of the significant application of paint to
the canvas, is so close, so indivisible, that the
painter can be said, in a telling phrase of Samuel
Alexander, to 'mix his mind with his material'.

We are here back once again to the mature artist,
in seeking for a clear example of the demonstration
of aesthetic or artistic sensitivity. But the same
argument could be applied to a teacher watching one
of his pupils paint: he could see, and if he wanted
to, assess, his pupil's aesthetic sensitivity. A
competent Inspector or External Examiner could do
the same (let us hope unknown to the pupil and -
hypothetically - from behind an unknown-to-the-pupil
-one-way-screen!).

And there is no question but that the same thing
applies to our critical appreciation of the finished
work presented to us, whether of a Master or of a
pupil in school. There is a long tradition of criticism of the Masters. It is true that there is always a subjective factor in the aesthetic perception
of a given work of art. Each person must become
aware of the work in a way which is in part irreduc-
ibly private. His 'interpretation', his reaction to
the work seen for the first time, and of which he has
heard no previous comment, is something quite personal to him. And if half a dozen other people are
present together under the same conditions in the
same room, in silent contemplation, there will be
half a dozen such private reactions. Because of
this undoubted fact, many people have said that since
these experiences are so indubitably private, the
appreciation of art is a purely personal and private
matter: it is all 'subjective': there is 'no
arguing about tastes'. But of course we do, not
merely utter our private opinions, but do argue

about our so-called aesthetic 'tastes', as we do
not argue with a friend who prefers tea whilst we
prefer coffee. In fact, the word 'taste' is quite
misleading and begs the question because when it
refers to coffee or tea it is pointing to a purely
private and personal set of sensations located in
the body and not to the particular qualities of the
coffee or tea. But when we are studying a picture,
it is the very complex and interrelated qualities
of the picture we see which we concentrate upon.
We certainly have sensations or other quite private
experiences, but these are subsidiary to something
quite different, namely judgements, and judgements
not about our own private states, but about the
picture as we see it. Furthermore, though our individual experiences of the picture have, as we have
been saying, their private and personal side, there
is much that through speech and perhaps gestures or
other communicative expressions which we can convey
to others of our judgments. Several people - let
us assume intelligent, aesthetically sensitive,
experienced, willing both to speak and to listen -
several people can discuss, not just their own sensations, but the qualities of the picture before
them. This is critical appreciation, and it is here
a social thing, as in one sense developed criticism
has always been. Each person must, at any rate to
begin with, deliver himself of his own private judgment. But these judgments are as it were thrown into
the common pool of discourse, and each can learn
from all the others as well as give to them. First
impressions, early intuitions, tend to be very partial, inadequate. Renewed intuitions, given substance
and enriched content through discussion - and of
course the reading of good criticism - these are the
product of competent criticism. It is in this way
that we pass towards a very considerably objective
understanding of art. The objectivity of art is of
course not like the objectivity of science which is
relatively impersonal in its statements, with feeling and subjective impression as far as possible
cast aside, with repeatable and transpersonal empirical tests. The objectivity, the standards of
testing successful or unsuccessful, good or bad,
art - these are matters not of pure intellect or
impersonal empirical testing, but of thinking in

which feeling has an indispensable part to play.
Or better, feeling and thinking of art are so unit-
ed, so fused together that they are one. The objectivity of judgments of art is never in any strict
sense _proved_; there is always a certain openness
about them. But there is, given time and a growing
body of sensitive and knowledgeable judgment, what
may be called a convergence towards objectivity.

All this - objectivity of judgment - applies to
school art, given trained, knowledgeable, discerning
teachers - and examiners. School art _can_ be judged,
with some degree of objectivity - though given the
variation in the qualities of teachers and inspectors
and examiners, and the short time given for making
judgments, there is a greater element of contin-
gency in it. I will not attempt to enlarge upon this,
or to exagerate it - for the important point to be
stressed is that school art _can_ with some measure of
objectivity be judged and assessed.

But there is another question which does worry some
- perhaps a good many - art teachers. Perhaps art
can be fairly assessed. But _should_ it be?

Before I attempt to comment on this, we ought to
remind ourselves that there are several other factors involved in the total picture of art and art
education. There are technical skills, knowledge
of and about the materials, of the various media,
awareness of the historical background of art, with
at least some broad background knowledge of art
history and its cultural setting. Without some
skills, without any know-that and know-how of the
media, the making of art would be, to say the least
of it, greatly hampered. And although it is certainly possible for a potentially gifted artist to start
from 'scratch', as it were, we could hardly call him
a 'well educated' person if he simply had no knowledge at all of the work of other artists and of a
background of history stretching right back to the
history of man. There is not much doubt that such
auxilliary, or background knowledge in a school
pupil _could_ be assessed; but the other question here
arises too: _should_ skills, know-that, know-how, or

knowledge-about historical background be required in
art education, either as separate factors or as integral parts of art making and art criticism?

First the question of the criticism and assessment of
art work made in school. There is no automatic inference from the legitimacy of the criticism of established professional artists, to its legitimacy in
schools. As we have agreed, the purpose in schools
is not to turn out artists, but to initiate them into
the experience of art making and discriminating enjoyment of given art. And it can be said that the
tender shooting plant needs protection and nourish-
ment, to be allowed to grow, without critical interference from outside, without assessing, measuring,
and above all competing. I have great sympathy with
the feelings behind this conviction. But I think it
is unrealistic and suffers from the analogy with the
growing plant. Human beings do not grow in the pre-
ordained way that plants do. They have to learn, and
learn by intelligent entry into the culture in which
they are born. Art as we have seen is not a purely
private matter: it is, _inter alia_, a making of something in a 'public' medium, which can be shared with
others and can gain from the opinions of others,
whether fellow pupils or more experienced teachers.
I certainly would not force a shy child or adolescent
against his will to expose himself and his work pre-
maturely: but he ought, I think, to be ready to consider it in the light of friendly criticism, in the
first instance of a teacher. It is not unnatural to
want to know how one is 'getting on'; and self criticism under guidance is an intrinsic element in
learning. A further stage may be to listen, perhaps
in the moderating presence of the teacher, to the
comments of his peers and in turn to offer comments
on their work. This is all on the road to learning
discriminating critical appreciation.

Everything, I am assuming, takes place within the
art-classroom situation, and under the guidance of a
good teacher - and on his or her qualities almost
everything depends.

But what about public examinations, and external examiners? Here the patterns of examining and of the

relations between internal teachers and external examiners vary so greatly that it would be difficult
even for a person who has had wide experience of such
things to generalise. As I personally have had very
little experience of the examining of practical art
and am not in fact professionally qualified to be
such an examiner, my opinions here would be pretty
worthless. I will only say that I can see very
clearly the great dangers of quick assessments by
purely external examiners of large quantities of work,
and the need for proper and sympathetic consultation
between the external examiner and the class teacher
who knows not only the productions of the pupils under
him, but the pupils themselves - as of course the external examiner cannot know them. Without sensitive
and intelligent co-operation great harm can be done.
But this in itself does not establish a case against
external examiners and public examinations in practical art. Public examinations in practical art are
bound to go on. Broadly speaking, I think it is
right that they should.

About the assessment of visual-art-criticism I see no
special difficulty. Reproductions (e.g.) or pictures
hitherto unseen can be presented under examination
conditions. The difficulties of some parts of examining the criticism of literature, for example, where
there are set books and it is possible for examinees
to parrot opinions read up beforehand, need not a-
rise. There is no reason why some of the techniques
of art criticism mentioned briefly earlier should not
be practised fruitfully under examination conditions.

I have done no more than mention so far the practical
skills involved in art-making, or of the testing of
knowledge-about - knowledge about techniques and materials, knowledge about art-history. Should there
be, can there be, separate testing of skills, for example? Or should any assessment of skills in the
manipulation or use of a medium in, say, painting, be
regarded simply as an item integral in the judgment
of the work as a whole? It is a difficult question.
In music examinations, for instance, or in dance,
technical proficiency can be marked, as such. Scales
and exercises, sight reading, control of body movements. Could one say the same thing of the assess-

ment of drawing (or perhaps even of the manipulation
of oil or water colour)? I think the answer depends
on how one thinks of the relations of these skills to
the aesthetic making of art itself. It seems pretty
clear that the examining and marking of scales and
exercises, or of the control of movement in dance, is
an assessing of some of the conditions of good art
making - in these two examples, of artistic performance. One can't play a difficult piece of music
without technical skill, or dance well a choreo-
graphed dance without the finest control. But skills
are never enough to make art: and if skills are separately assessed, the assessment is of skills, not
assessment of art as such. The same I think applies
to drawing. To be able to draw well is an asset to
an artist - though not everyone would say that it is
essential, say to a painter or a sculptor, or a
potter. But the ability to draw well is not, as such
art, and the assessment of drawing is not, as such,
the assessment of art. There is perhaps a stronger
general case for learning to draw - that it is useful
in all sorts of ways outside art: but this is irrelevant so far as art education is concerned.

My very tentative conclusion on all this is that in
the visual arts, and when we keep firmly in mind that
it is visual with which we are mainly concerned, it
is sounder to assess the various skills involved not
as skills, qua skills (as they may do in music or
dance), but as inseparable aspects of good art making. Moreover, there may even be a danger in considering (say) skill in drawing as such. Drawing can
be of different kinds; and the strictly accurate,
realistic drawing which may be useful in some fields
(including sometimes art) may be quite out of keeping
with the general style of this or that piece of art.
The aesthetic unity of the work of art ought to dom-
inate everything else.

I have mentioned history of art. About this I will
only say that if well taught and intelligently
learned, some historical knowledge of art seems a
sine qua non of liberal education in the arts. There
are many ways of teaching it, into which I cannot go.
Only one thing must be made clear. History of art is
in part necessarily factual, and one cannot know

anything about the history of art without acquiring
knowledge of many facts. There is of course nothing
wrong with this. But if it stayed there it would not
be history of art except in the most superficial
sense. It only becomes truly history of art if all
the time it is an aesthetically critical-appreciative
study, a learning to look, study, consider, to make
thoughtful maturer judgments. This may seem too obvious to say. But unfortunately some history of art
is taught and learned in anything but this way. And
good teaching of art history in schools is unfortunately too rare. It is high time that the situation
be reviewed.

I won't try to sum up an already long lecture. You
will gather that, with one or two reservations, I do
think that various components of art education can be
assessed, and ought to be, if we are to claim that
there are any standards at all in art education. But
of course always, every time, it depends on the way
it is done, and on the qualities - knowledge, training, experience, skill, sympathy and understanding of
those, teachers or external examiners, who participate
in it. No rules or regulations can ever be a substitute for enlightened human insight. If that is a
commonplace, it is a commonplace which is often forgotten.

I referred at the beginning of this paper to misgivings and fears about the 'monitoring' of the arts,
and the 'Assessment of Performance Units'. They are
natural and proper: anyone who cares about aesthetic
education must have felt them. When one has the arts
in mind, some of the language of the DES Report on
Education (Number 93, August 1978) which may apply
very well to the assessment of, say, mathematics, the
sciences, or languages, is utterly inapplicable to
the arts. With the arts in mind, and the danger of
transferring categories which may be quite appropriate in other subjects, to the arts, I felt some
alarm, even horror. On the other hand, though there
are dangers of things getting into wrong hands; we
cannot just assume this. To some extent it is a fear
of the unknown: we do not yet know exactly how
'monitoring' in the arts will be carried out and im-
plemented. And, on a main issue, I cannot think that

a survey of art education over the country is, in itself objectionable in principle.

I will only comment on two, conceptual, points.

(1)   Assessment of pupils' education in the arts
by examiners, and assessment by Inspectors of art
teaching, is no new thing.   We do mark degrees of
achievement, literally or numerically. In doing so
there is an assumption of 'better' or 'worse'; there
are assumptions about what has, and what has not
been accomplished in pupils' work.   We know that
there is no infallibility, in ideas of what 'good' or
'bad' art should be, or in examiners' particular
judgments about this or that work. But judgment,
assessment, marking, all happen; and (fallible)
judgment is basic. It seems necessary to stress this
banal and obvious point, because one of the fears
about assessment when it takes the form of, or is
called, 'monitoring' seems to be that monitoring is
somehow reductive of judgment to some grading scale
which registers or expresses it, necessarily in impersonal terms. But judgment of quality (whatever
doubts we may have about the varying competences of
judgment) is logically prior to impersonal - say
numerical - recording. If, in the hands of people
who, knowing nothing about the special nature of art,
it became some formula-substitute for judgment, con-
taining, perhaps, a list of criteria which could be
ticked off one by one - this would be the 'end' of
education in the arts. But we are not entitled to
make such an assumption. Recording, as such, does
not interfere with the proper exercise of art, or
mechanically freeze the life of art into a formula.
Measuring in itself doesn't destroy: only a foolish
use of it could.

(2)   But there is, in some people's minds, a
deeper objection, which lies behind the fear of a
particular kind of monitoring. It is the radical
objection to any assessment of art. I hope that I
have, in the body of the paper, said something which
tells against this objection.   It is a fallacy, I
think, inherent in some extreme forms of 'expression-
ism'. Good art teachers very rightly respect the
freedom of the pupil to have his own private

subjective life, his own personal feelings and emotions, and, in art, they have a respect for his own
personal way of seeing and doing things. This is of
the utmost importance; and it goes along with the
pupils' right of freedom not to show his work for
public display if, after suggestion, he still does
not want to. But this is only one side of the picture. It is, as I believe and have suggested, quite
wrong to suppose that art <u>is</u> merely self-expression
or 'expression of the emotions' - a purely private
affair. Art is also something which can be expressed
and embodied in public media, which can be aesthetically perceived, and shared, with other people. As
such, it is fairly open to critical appraisement,
judgment, sometimes assessment. I think that respect
for the personal, private, individual, right as it is
on one side of teaching art, goes radically wrong
when it leads to the supposition that works of art
(as well as some other products of art education
which I have mentioned) should not be assessed, or at
least be open to assessment.

Assessment and Evaluation in the Arts

DAVID ASPIN

I am particularly concerned with the question of
"Assessment and Evaluation" in the Arts. I begin
from the theme of this conference, which is "Relevance
and Responsibility in the Arts". Both of these terms
are found in and associated with much of the recent
thinking about the curriculum, and they pose special
problems for the Arts. Some of these new curriculum
pronouncements are such as are contained in: Aspects
of the Curriculum; A View of Curriculum; and Curriculum 11 to 16 - all probably emanating from the
speech that was delivered by the then Prime Minister
at Ruskin College, Oxford, in October 1976. The lat-
est publication in this series - Aspects of the Secondary Education Curriculum - has been criticized by
many and, with especial trenchancy, vigour and devastating candour by Malcolm Ross (1980) is one that
poses a particularly serious threat for Arts education. For in that paper, the Arts are relegated to
the role of "second-class citizen"; it is clear that,
in the view of those who wrote that pamphlet, they
are "frills" on the curriculum, rather than - as we
think they should be - fundamentals.

"Relevance" and "responsibility" were key notions in
the new curriculum thinking, the chief thrust of which
is associated with that model of education, educabil-
ity and educational achievement that is derived from
the economic sphere. Sir Arnold Weinstock, in an
article in the Times Educational Supplement which
preceded the Prime Minister's Ruskin College speech
by a few weeks, was one of those industrialists who
articulated a demand for accountability - but this
was 'accountability' conceived in terms of an

economic model. There does not appear, to us at any
rate, to be so much difference between the pronuncia-
mentos of the gnomes of industry on the minimum
desiderata of education and that of the view of the
curriculum embodied in Aspects of the Secondary Education Curriculum, emanating from the gnomes of Eliz-
abeth House. A feature of this notion of accountability is the idea that teachers should in some way
or other be able to give a quantifiable account - cash
value - of what it is that they do. Particularly in
times of monetarist political philosophies, the demand for hard returns in almost financially access-
ible terms has grown apace and is not, I think, likely to diminish in the currently prevailing economic
climate, where committed monetarists are in control
of our public institutions and all that goes with
them.

I mean not to make a political point here but an anti-
economic one. My point is a logical one, to do with
the inappropriateness of applying economic criteria
to the assessment of something which is not only
strongly resistant to economic demands but is ab in-
itio recalcitrant to them; the application of such
criteria is, I believe, categorically inappropriate.

That is not to say, however, that teachers are not or
should not be 'responsible' or 'accountable'. Why
that is so emerges very rapidly, I think, from the
grounds and nature of the teacher's authority and the
idea that the teacher is in his position only, so to
speak, on sufferance. To employ Peters' distinction
- the teacher is someone who is placed in authority
by parents, who delegate their powers to him, pro
tempore, on the grounds of his being an authority on
certain matters, subjects and areas of knowledge
thought by them to be of value and worthwhile trans-
mitting to their children (1966, 1973). And the
exercise of his authority as a teacher is only justi-
fiable so long as he conforms to those normative
criteria. The teacher will be empowered by them to
act as someone with special knowledge, expertise or
skill, that gives him the status of a person qualified to impart or transmit to their children or to
initiate them into those bodies of cognitive content
and practical skills that are presumed to be held

worthwhile by the parents who are willing to expose
and subject their children to those processes.

Clearly I am talking here about public education in
secular institutions supported and funded by the
State - though there is no reason for private schools
of any kind to be excepted from what I say. What is
at issue is the question of people seeking to educate
their young according to their own beliefs, in their
own ways and for their own values. What I say assumes that the teacher, under the sufferance and with
the permission of constituent members or representa-
tives of the Common Will, will act, in the time hon-
oured phrase, 'in loco parentis', to introduce children to certain activities, progress and success in
which he will promote, plan for, monitor and assess.
So ultimately, when he is called upon to do so (as he
can be in principle at any time) he will be able to
render an account to those who have employed him for
that purpose, of his exercise of stewardship of the
parents' own role and function during the time when
they were otherwise engaged in either bringing up
other children, continuing in their own interests, or
otherwise earning their own living. Thus the idea of
the teacher's authority is clearly the principal pin
upon which our considerations of the problems of
assessment and accountability rest (Sockett et al,
1980). In our investigating these topics there are
at least four areas that are problematic: there are
problems to do with the work of the artist; problems
to do with the activity of the artist; problems to do
with the assessor's activity of perceiving, appreciating and judging; and problems that lie in the
process of assessment itself. I shall try to say
something about each of these.

Why these things are problematic emerges from a consideration of the character of what it is that artists are doing when they are creating their own artifacts; who it is that is doing it; what counts as a
work of art; and who reckons it to be a success - the
four areas of work; worker; judge; and the process of
judgement.

I begin with the problems of the work itself. What,
we may ask, is a work of art if indeed there can be

such a thing? How might we recognize one? Further
to this: if there are works of art, can they be
judged? And if so, by what criteria? For we are all
well aware of a number of aphorisms and opinions
which are to be found in the vocabulary of at least
some people and at least some art teachers: "Beauty
lies in the eye of the beholder"; "one man's meat is
another man's poison", and so on. Such sentences are
often symptomatic of the idea that works of art are
unique, are individual, are specific to the time, the
occasion and the worker. To put a philosophical
gloss upon it, it has been said that there is a profound mistake in traditional aesthetics in attempting
to move from the particular to the general; when the
philosopher does this he has gone the wrong way (Cf
Hampshire, 1954; Kennick, 1965).

From this kind of thinking is often then extracted
the conclusion that, because in talk about the Arts
one cannot move from the general to the particular,
the   view   that   aesthetics   is a sui generis form
of discourse, in which meaningful statements can be
made and of which proper analytical accounts can be
given, collapses. There is no point, such an opinion
holds, in attempting to wrestle with something which
is, after all, nothing more than a large gas-filled
bag.

This form of extreme subjectivism in aesthetics is,
in my view, quite as silly as the sorts of subjectivism that one comes across in ethics. It is simply
not the case in moral matters that hitting an old
lady over the head with a stick or indulging in an
act of gang rape on an underage girl is something one
can take or leave as a matter of completely subjective preference. Similarly with aesthetics: I ven-
ture to suggest that the situation in aesthetics is
analogous - that our judgements of works of art are
simply not something that one can take or leave.
The justification for my taking this view rests upon
considerations arising from the "public language"
argument (Wittgenstein, 1953); that is to say, works
of art are, in my view, 'objective' in that they are,
in some sense, "propositions" in a public language
form (Hirst, 1973), that are put forward within one
of the human worlds of interpersonal discourse and

that are therefore capable of being understood and
appraised in terms of the logic of all the various
kinds of meaning and signification that together constitute the totality of interpersonal communication.

I must make it quite clear that when I talk about
works of art being communications put forth for aesthetic intelligibility and appraisal in public language, I do not restrict myself to one kind of language only - the oral. The possibility of making
propositions in the aesthetic realm is not limited to
the merely discursive. If it were, there would be no
need for artists to paint pictures, sculptors to
sculpt statues, and musicians to compose symphonies,
because all the manifold and myriad areas of meaning
that such works embody and encapsulate would otherwise be capable of being expressed by the spoken word
- which manifestly they are not. There is a story of
Schumann, who had composed a new work and then played
it to a friend in its totality. At the end of the
piece, his friend, who had listened in wonder, said
to him "That's marvellous, Robert, but what does it
mean?" "Ah", said Robert, "it means this!" - and
played it again.

So a work of art is objective, is open to appraisal.
But the next question is: by what kind of test, and
from what kind of paradigm or perspective do we seek
to understand and appreciate it? We could, for example, operate on the basis of an expressionist
stance, in which we maintain that art is the expression of emotion; or we may take the idea of art as representation as being the correct account of the
function of works of art. Then too there is the art
of socialist realism - art as the manifestation of
particular stages in the process of historical materialism and dialectics. Clearly, the particular
perspective that one adopts in the evaluation and
assessment of a work of art will crucially determine
the kind of judgements that one believes it will be
possible to make about its objectivity. This is,
then, a second problem in this first area of consideration:

   (1)(a) Can a work of art be assessed?
   (1)(b) If so, by what kinds of criteria; from
what kinds of different paradigm?, and

(1)(c) What sort of arguments can be employed for bringing to bear one paradigm rather than another? Why, for example, should we try to view _Guernica_ or _David_ from representationalist, expressivist, materialist or realist perspectives? Why should one be held to be more meaningful and more valuable than another?

These questions of the criteria and the justifiability of the criteria that we use for assessment in attempting to make some sort of informed appreciation and judgement of what we take to be an aesthetic object (not necessarily a work of art) - these are all areas of problems of the first kind that I delineated above.

The second kind of problem area I located in the work of the artist. What is the artist "doing" when he is doing his business of producing photographs or symphonies or major works such as a mural on a wall or even something as apparently simplistic and superficial as a plastic garden gnome? What is he trying to do? And, come to that, is it important that he be _trying_ to "do" anything at all? There is a story about Debussy, that at one time he was producing an orchestral work "against the clock". So pressing was his deadline that, more or less as he finished one page, the paper was snatched off him with the ink still wet and taken straight off to the copyists, and then parcelled out to the orchestra, which then got busy on the rehearsal. So much so, that the final page was only produced about two days before the final rehearsal, to which Debussy was himself invited. According to the story, such had been the speed of work that Debussy had no time to put dynamic marks on the piece and, crucially, metronome marks. So he went to the final rehearsal, the maestro sat in the front row and the piece was begun. The violins were suddenly aware that a very troubled expression had come over the maestro's face; their music slowly subsided, and the orchestra collapsed into one of those dreadful cataclysms that only an orchestral rehearsal can be, as they realized that something had, apparently, gone horribly wrong. And the conductor turned around and said, "Maitre Debussy, is something the matter?" And he is reported to have said, "Yes,

you are playing it twice as. fast as I intended it to
be played - but carry on; you are right!" This
story, whether true or not, is a devastating expose
of what is called the "intentionalist" fallacy.

What is the artist trying to do? Even if we knew it,
would it matter? This is another area of problem.
Does the fact that some Russian ballerina's father
was a Siberian train-driver have anything to do with
the aesthetic appraisal that we make of her floor
exercises in the dance? Some people answer yes,
others no. The artist, then, and the problem of the
possibility of our ever being able to elicit his intention, the question of the feasibility of our in-
spection of his motives - the philosophical problem
of knowledge of other people's minds - intrudes at
this point.

Supposing that we are talking about locating the artist at a particular point in the process of his artistic development: What then? What particular stage
of an artist's development is he actually at, in his
own art form? What are we to make of that? Let us
take, for example, the very early compositions of
Johann Sebastian Bach - the works he produced before
the age of 18; and contrast these, in Mendelssohn's
case, with the works he produced after ·the age of 18.
Both, it seems, are largely disvalued because they
represent something that is not held to be "true" of
their finest creations. But how would we know what
these were?

This merits more extended treatment and I shall return later to the question of the truth as a criterion of assessment in the arts. But the problems that
arise concerning the process of the artist's own development are critical in another important respect
as well. In the "Introduction" that Dmitri
Schostakovitch penned to his Fifth Symphony, he described it as "a Soviet artist's reply to just criticism". But in answering a criticism from the
"official" organ of Soviet musicians' thinking,
Schostakovitch was clearly operating within and responding in terms of the perspective of dialectical
materialism. 'That is all very well for dialectical
materialists', some realist or some expressionist

may say. 'But, listen to this dreadful symphony;
listen to the banality of that dreadful brass; listen
to the fact that he never succeeds in doing anything
that is not, ultimately, bathos; there is no real expression of emotion there.' Here one would have
somebody operating from within a different paradigm
and attempting to make an informative appraisal of
somebody else working in a radically different paradigm - the two of which are mutually exclusive. What
then? How then is it legitimate to make any appraisal at all of what another artist is doing? For the
problem here is the status, justifiability and com-
patibility of alternative and competing paradigms in
terms of which we articulate our aesthetic judgements.

Having talked about the person whose productions are
being assessed in this way, we now come onto the person making the assessments - the assessor. There are
a number of problems here. To begin with, we have to
ask, what is the status of his authority as an assessor? Is one, for example, going to or obliged to
take any notice of views of the Mrs. Grundys of this
world on arts and works of art? Who think that the
sentiment "I know what I like, and what I like is
that blue-faced girl that hangs over my fireplace"
counts as a valid aesthetic judgement? I came across
a space once, in a beautiful room in the Stedelijk
in Amsterdam, and all there was on the wall was a
little plaque. On this was written: 'PROJECT FOR
VISIBLE NEGATION - A SPACE FOR NO CHAIR.' And there
came in a large party of tourists, from whom one
heard all sorts of guffaws, outrage, bewilderment and
the rest, that were being ejaculated, eructed or articulated when they came to this.

It is, I think, about time that people who are "on
the inside of" the Arts stood up against the notion
that the "gut" reactions of the ignorant, the misin-
formed, the deluded or the malicious have to be
accepted as valid judgements of the meaning and value
of works of art. Mathematicians are scornful of
people whose numeracy is not sufficiently well developed to enable them even to understand the workings
of a calculator. Scientists shake their heads when
people are unable to understand the technical arguments for or against fluoridation of water supplies.

Religious experts are equally dismayed, though perhaps in a very much more charitable way, when they
try to explain to "lay" people such difficult concepts as that of the Trinity or the Immaculate Conception. Why, then, should it be thought in the lay
mind that, when it comes to our appreciation in and
of the Arts, anybody's view will do as well as that
of the experts? Such a view strikes me as a plain
misconception; certainly it has always failed to evoke
any kind of a serious response in me. Just as people
can be innumerate or unscientific, so can people be
illiterate in the Arts. This is one of the first
things that we must establish, then. When I talk
about 'assessors' in the Arts, I am not talking about
the illiterate, the uninformed or the ignorant. I
make no apology for this; for, just as in the case of
teachers, so too in the case of artists and their
work - I am talking about the status of authority -
the authority that enables one to make a critical,
rigorous and informed judgment of somebody else's
best level of work. It behoves the assessor to
attempt to be as informed, critical, rigorous and
able at the same level as near to that of the artist
as he can, if he is going to make any sort of full
account and valid assessment of it. Because it is
upon such competence that his authority to do so
rests. We must therefore next ask, what kinds of
knowledge do we need in making this kind of judgment?
And the answer would seem to be, that we require a
large number.

With all diffidence I should like to advance the view
that, in our judgments of works of art, which I pre-
sume we will have to make as teachers in and of the
arts (since by definition teaching will entail the
continual making of assessments of some kind or
other), there are various kinds of knowledge involved. There will be a technical kind of knowledge
to begin with, as, for example, that which relates to
the chemical composition of a glaze in ceramics, or
the correct suspension of pigment in emulsion. There
will be an amount of historical knowledge too, such
as, for example, what were the precise nature and
number of the musical forces that Bach had at his
disposal in the Thomas-Kirche in Leipzig in the
1720s. There will be sociological considerations
about the observed tendencies groups exhibit to the

making of judgements of a certain kind of works that
are available to them. There will be psychological
kinds of knowledge to do with the perceptual effects
of after-glow and after-image, as, for example, in
the connoisseurship of good wine. There will certainly be anthropological knowledge: the ritual
function of masks in the theatre, for example. There
will be a large amount of scientific knowledge to do
with matters such as perspective. There may be some
mathematical knowledge, having to do with such notions as symmetry and proportion, and certainly in
Pythagorean tuning terms, in the idea of the ratio of
scales and the ways one tunes a chord. There will be
an amount of philosophical knowledge required too,
because the student and appraisor will have to know
what it is that he is judging, and by what criteria;
what counts as an admissible piece of work in a particular genre. Maybe, too, there will be an amount of
what Hirst calls 'interpersonal' knowledge (Hirst and
Peters, 1970) - the way in which what some existen-
tialists call "Soul-contact" takes place, that kind
of knowledge which Martin Buber sees in the "I-Thou"
relationship - a relationship subsisting not only
between the appraisor and the artist but also between
the appraisor and the work of art. This makes appraising a work of art a process of conversation
(Reid, 1957) - a dialogue that goes on between the
various kinds of bearers of meanings in a work of art
that leads to the possibility in our appraisals of
aesthetic objects of what Sonia Greger described as
"stripping away the layers" of meaning (Greger, 1972).
For in this way, the perceiver and judge of a work of
art comes to have and to enjoy more, and more rich
dimensions and kinds of meaningfulness are added to
his understanding of the world in terms of his contact with the bearers of such possibilities.

The appraisor of the arts will certainly have to have
some degree of competence and authoritative standing
in a number, if not all, of these areas of cognition
and communication. But as well as - and not instead
of - these, he will have to be well educated in and
able to operate according to the canons of that mode
of awareness and understanding of the world that we
call "the aesthetic" - that mode, the characteristic
features of which consist in its disinterested

contemplation of objects in accordance with criteria
of what, according to some theory or other, counts as
excellent, and as giving some kind of satisfaction to
the perceiver and the appraiser (Strawson, 1974).   An
able and informed assessor, whose judgments will com-
mand our respect, will have to have all of this.   And
it will be this <u>knowledge</u> of his that gives him the
right, the power and the understanding to judge.   It
will be, as it were, within the community constituted
by the discourse and the conversations of those who
participate and engage in it (equivalent to the community of scholars in the sciences, or mathematics,
or philosophy) that such judgments will have standing
and warrantable assertability.   There is a similar,
equal community of the artistic world;   and the mar-
velous thing about the artistic community is that it
is as rich and variegated in its polyphony as is the
world of the sciences, in which we have not only the
single disciplines of biology, chemistry and physics,
but where people work in between areas, as in bio-
chemistry and biophysics.   So it is too in the Arts.
For in the Arts we have not only the rich mosaic of
the language and literature of the arts, but also
those of the subsidiary constitutive disciplines –
the enactive, the oral, the visual, the musical and
so on and so forth.   I hold that the community constituted by the arts is as rich and diverse and
variegated and as of equal authoritative standing as
the world of the sciences.   It is perhaps time that
so much was claimed for it – clearly and unambiguously (Aspin, 1980).

It will be objected that there is much less controversy in the sciences than in the Arts.   For example,
a mathematician in Russia can talk relatively the
same language as a mathematician in Buenos Aires;   a
scientist in Ottawa can talk to a scientist in Omsk.
Try going around any of the galleries, even in London
it will be said, and look at the various perspectives
that there are, the various competing theories as to
what even constitutes an agreed pronouncement in the
arts, much less authoritative ones to which we could
all with respect defer.

It is at this point that we have frankly to face the
problem of the varying ideological perspectives in

the Arts. From what standpoint does an assessor
judge as he does, and why? How can he account for
and defend the judgments and appraisals that he
makes? It is here that we have to be conscious of
ourselves, to admit and indeed to see that in our
assessments in and of the arts, the judgments that we
make are quite clearly a function of the preconcep-
tions that we, as particular judges, bring to the
works of particular artists - and of those that they
brought to their creating of them.

In his chapter in <u>Values and Evaluation in Education</u>
(edited by Roger Straughan and Jack Wrigley) Fraser
Smith (1980) produces a typology of art teachers in
schools, and of the various perspectives from which
people operate, both as teachers and as assessors.
There are the "High Priests", subdivided into 'connoisseurs', 'magicians' and 'mystics'; there are
the "Technocrats", subdivided into the 'engineers'
and 'designers'; there are Social Workers; there
are the Anomics; there are the Semiologists; and,
last and greatest in number, there are the Peda-
gogues. What Smith ultimately produces is a typology
of the various values, each of which is critically
determinative of the appraisals that such different
groups of assessors and disseminators of the arts
make of what is offered to them or what they perceive. He writes, for example, of some art teachers
whom we can best identify as "Magicians". They value,
above everything else, the creative act. Their version of the nature of art emphasizes independence,
secrecy, mystery and the ritual, personal intensity,
the mysterious nature of the art, the ineffable
nature of artworks and the <u>essential unteachability</u>
<u>of art.</u> Those whom he calls "Technocrats", by con-
trast, are all for 'efficiency'; Bloom is their god.
They specify behavioural objectives in modules and
units and courses; they believe that processes and
outcomes in art should be subject to rational and
logical analysis; they plan their teaching in terms
of a prepared sequence of observable behavioural
changes and optimum recognizable solutions. They are
all for data. Their personal promotion lies in what
they allege to be the <u>measurability</u> of arts. 'Social
Workers', by contrast, he maintains, are all for the
therapeutic value of the arts; expression of emotion,

freedom, love and warmth. Such people give their
grades for effort, attitude and social adjustment.

But if the Social Worker is the sort of
art teacher who murmurs, 'Now doesn't
that make you feel better?' at the end
of a session in which it would appear
to an observer that assorted young thugs
of both sexes had spent eighty obscenity
-laden minutes drawing or painting
scenes of appalling violence in which
swastika-bedecked Hell's Angels or
blood-dripping vampires go about all
their too well-imagined business, then
this is not for him a solicitous enquiry but a statement of faith.

The Anomic, by contrast, places the main value of art
in the opportunity it offers for aggression and host-
ility to the prevailing ethos and social climate.

No doubt some teachers will find this kind of writing
not only disturbing but even outrageously controversial, written with a particular point of view to
put forward. Nevertheless such comments on the world
of art teaching are worth reading for showing the
essential point that appraisals in the arts are very
much more subject to and a direct function of the
particular perspective or paradigm from which we approach it. Perhaps in this respect the world of the
arts, the community of the arts, might seem to be
dissimilar to that of the scientists. It is not too
dissimilar, however, since none who can remember the
acrimonies of the debate concerning the nature of the
electron in the 1930s between Heisenberg and Schröd-
inger, and the lengths to which they went in critical
disputation, will think that some of the things that
we hear in places like museums, art galleries, concert halls, or art schools, are at all unusual. At
all events, we see that this is a particular area of
problem in the arts - the nature of, and the justifiability of adopting the particular perspective
which lends status to the authority of the appraiser's
judgments in and of the arts. To this I wish to return shortly.

My final area of problem concerns the process of
assessment itself. What is an 'assessment'? What
information can be held to be relevant to it? What
goals are being specified and looked at? Why those
goals rather than some others? Why, for instance,
should we aim for 'therapy' rather than 'expression'?
How is our information to be gathered? How is it to
be reported, and crucially, for what purposes? In
other words, one of the issues that is most problematic, when we come to tackle the problems of assessment in the Arts, is the problem of assessment itself.

In tackling this issue, some people might argue that
a good starting point would be to try to work out and
give some definitions. I do not believe that there
is much point or purpose in such an enterprise. For
there are profound philosophical arguments against
attempting to arrive at unambiguous definitions, of
the sort with which we are all too familiar. Faced
with such problems and arguments I wish simply to
stipulate and state what I shall take assessment to
be. I believe that, at rock bottom, assessment is a
process or activity of attempting to get information
from someone or some source about somebody or something. As a result of this process of information-
getting what emerges is a judgment - an estimation of
either a factual kind, that is to say a judgment in
terms of a description of an object; or an estimation
of the worth or value of something and a fixing of
that object of assessment, where we are talking in
evaluative terms, relative to predetermined criteria
that are held to be relevant and specific to it.

Evaluation, I think, is for these reasons a similar
idea. Indeed, in the literature the two are often
used interchangeably. Evaluation in many accounts
means giving a value to, weighing up, making some
estimation or account of, weighing up all parts of
something so as to give some account of the 'state of
the art', in descriptive terms, or, in evaluative
ones, of its worthwhileness or functional utility.

Neither term, in so far as they are separable at all,
is to be confused with 'examination'. Examination I
take to mean a scrutiny or an enquiry into something,
simply to establish its present state, operation and

functioning by a particular <u>model</u> of assessment. In
other words, I do not equate examination of any kind
- CSE, O level, A level, CEE, or whatever - <u>with</u>
assessment. Examinations are <u>one</u> <u>form</u> of making
assessments. We must not confuse a whole area of activity with only one of its procedures; there are
other ways in which assessments can be made, and I
shall try shortly to say what some of these can be.

At this point I believe it important simply to distinguish between <u>descriptions</u>, the factual accounts
that we can make of a present state, level or standard of achievement (what a pupil has achieved, what
skills he has learned) - what some people call
"summative assessment" - and <u>judgmental assessment</u>
which is of a radically different kind. I wish, in
other words, to distinguish between "ticking off" the
<u>correct</u> answers to factual questions concerning
achievements which can in some way be measured (skill
(skills, additions to cognitive repertoire, increase
in vocabulary or stores of ideas, the ability to
handle a brush, the ability to use words); and the
<u>acceptable</u> answers to other kinds of questions and
demands, which require the skills and knowledge ac-
quired in these ways to be put to a use. Perhaps I
can best illustrate this by drawing an example from
my own earlier academic interests.

I can distinguish quite clearly between the sorts of
assessment one can make as to whether people are able
to translate English into Latin or Greek "correctly".
Here questions such as the following are pertinent:
are you able to handle a certain construction? Is
this an example of Ablative, Absolute, or Accusative
and Infinitive? With such questions one can correct
factual knowldge by means of a multiple choice test
or a simple substitution exercise; people's answers
are either right or wrong. There is no dubiety about
assessing answers to plain questions of fact: either
one knows that red traffic lights mean stop or one
doesn't. And of that sort of "achievement" one can
give a factual, descriptive account and mark it
straightforwardly right or wrong. This is one kind
of assessment we make of one's linguistic competence
in Latin. At University level, however, it is taken
for granted that one can handle Ablative, Absolutes,

Accusatives and Infinitives and similar sorts of
linguistic construction; the ultimate test of linguistic competence in a University setting is, can
one turn a piece of English prose or verse into an
imaginative, creative piece of writing, that is not
merely a <u>pastiche</u> or what Horace or Cicero might have
written but is in fact a creative endeavour in the
use of the language itself, that brings about a
heightened sense of awareness and a greater sense of
illumination, such that in some way the syntax and
grammar of the language has been used so as to give
rich kinds of meaning and satisfaction to a receiver
and spectator. Competence in that sort of enterprise
requires the bringing to bear of powers of judgment
and criticism of an <u>appreciative and evaluative</u> kind.

By 'evaluative' I wish to underline the primary concern of such 'creative' activities with the making
and application of judgments of value - estimating
the work, desirability, or the utility of an object
or performance, to be judged on the presence or ab-
sence of certain features, within a particular class
of comparison, that count as "excellent" in some way,
and on a scale of ranking with other similar objects
(Najder, 1975). An <u>action</u> towards another person,
for example, may be counted as more or less 'moral'in
comparison with other actions judged on the application of such criteria, as to, for example, whether
that was the 'honourable' thing to do. Now judgments
of 'honour' and the like are not all-or-nothing
things; they are not once-and-for-all affairs; they
are not matters of a simple discrimination between
white and black. Judgments - of honour or of anything
else of that kind - operate on a sliding scale, in
accordance with one's criteria of what constitutes
honourableness, and, further, in accordance with the
particular moral perspective from which one is working when one makes such judgments.

So it is with our assessment of works of art. We
judge, in a ranking order, in accordance with certain
criteria of what counts as excellent for us, within a
particular class of comparison. I don't, for example,
try aesthetically to compare a sonnet with a cathedral and judge both, and it would be absurd to try to
analogize between a painting and a sculpture. The

criteria of 'correctness' in each <u>genre</u>, when we are
making aesthetic judgments about particular works of
art, are not exactly exclusive but they are not sus-
ceptible to analogization in this way.

I thus distinguish between factual assessments and
judgmental assessments. I now wish to go further and
to say something about the kinds and processes of
assessment that people make of works of Art. I wish
now to distinguish between three kinds of assessment
that are and can be made in respect of any objects,
performances or processes. We distinguish, normally
speaking, between <u>normative</u> assessments, <u>criterial</u>
assessments and <u>developmental</u> assessments. So, for
example, in the marking of Latin sentences, it is
perfectly possible to produce right or wrong things.
At the top of an '0' level scale, there will be some
people who have got 100 out of 100 right answers; at
the bottom of that scale, there may be some people
who have succeeded in getting nothing right - 0 percent. That kind of assessment involves a <u>criterial</u>
judgment, obtained from the checking of answers a-
rising from consideration of what are the criteria of
correctness for, say, a conditional sentence in Latin, or a substitution exercise in quadratic equations
in mathematics. And there one is either right or
wrong, or more right or more wrong. On the basis
that one gets more and more of the criteria right,
one hundred percent answers are possible. But now
the oddity: at '0' level the application of such
criteria is restricted to the top twentieth percent-
ile of the educational population, that is to say, to
all those people who over against their peers, are at
least 80 percent <u>better</u>. The question is now a different one: how does one make a differentiating
judgment like that? Quite easily: take a class and
the one that's at the bottom of the scale of achievement on a criterial basis, we put at nought; the one
at the top of the same scale we put at 100. Then we
make a graph of a standard range of distribution, in
which the large mass will come in the middle.

The questions for <u>this</u> kind of "normative" distribution process are simple: what kind of discriminations
do we wish to make, on a ranking basis between the
performances of one member of a group and another?

How many percent of these candidates do we want to
assign to various distinct classes this year? And at
this point such considerations as these come in: last
year in the 'A' sub-class, it was 5.8%; the year before it was 3.6%; the year before that it was 8.7%.
One hears such comments as: "I think we've been a
bit lenient in the past; this year we'll restrict
the A's to 4.6% of the total". We then take a list
of candidates; establish that the cut-off point
comes at so many percent, and we can locate a candidate easily. Candidate X this year obtains 300 marks
and thus obtains first-class Honours. Last year he
would not have got a first. The year before that, he
would have been easily in the first category. In the
case of another candidate, we see that he obtains
298.8 marks. Thus he is awarded this year a Class II
Division One degree. This is what is meant by 'normative assessments'. They are judged on a sliding
scale, relative to each other - and to nothing else.

Is there anything wrong with this kind of assessment?
Some people say not, but my opinion is to the contrary. Quite apart from the moral defensibility of
such a procedure of treating people, there are major
technical criticisms to be made of it. Of these the
two chief ones are: (1) it fails to discriminate
effectively between the achievements of the vast
mass of the range of candidates, with particular respect to those who are located in the C's - the
middle range. There are not really that many A's and
E's, but there are a great many C's in the middle
range. The phenomenon that occurs then is that
"bunching" judgments are made.

An examiner can be simply told by his Examining Board
to produce so many piles according to a normal curve
of distribution. And when one has got this pile -
the C's - one can in turn sort out these and these
and these. But the whole pile will still be the big-
gest. And all the people in it C's. Differences of
individual achievements between whole ranges of candidates can be totally obliterated by this kind of
assessment.

But that is not the only criticism; there is another
one. In a work of artistic creation, such as the

writing of a Greek prose, for example, it is perfectly possible for me to write a certain kind of prose, which, judged in terms of certain <u>criteria</u>, will get me an A, and judged in other kinds of <u>criteria</u>, will get me an E. When the question arises as to where am I to be put relative to <u>all</u> other performances, most examiners compromise and give me a C. And this procedure strikes one as arbitrary, or unthinking – certainly requiring further justification. There is no such problem in justifying the sorts of criteria that we may properly apply; so the first thing that is wrong with normative assessments is the <u>imprecise</u> nature of the judgments that are made.

Secondly, however – and this is where I think it not unreasonable that moral judgments should come in – normative assessment emphasizes the <u>competitive</u> nature of examinations of this kind. To show this is a quite straightforward matter. In an examination which is marked normatively, on a normative curve, I am given the mark of 45%. So I then work very hard for the next six months and prepare myself for another test. Come the time of the test, I might have improved my performance by 100%. So has everybody else, however. So when the results come out, I am still given and placed at 45% in spite of the fact that, <u>against myself</u>, I have improved 100%. The only way in which, on normative marking, I can improve my performance, is by <u>outperforming</u> somebody above me and taking marks off him. Hence the emphasis on the competitive nature of the examination.

What I also find equally morally reprehensible in this kind of assessment is the emphasis on <u>failure</u>. Given any normative curve of distribution, there will be people who are seen as E's and D's, no matter how well they have performed on any <u>criterial</u> basis. Candidates who obtain 65% out of 100% <u>on a criterial basis</u> in a test, in which, say, the question happened to involve a simple substitution exercise for quadratic equation in maths, can be placed in the E grade, because everybody else performed overall so much better than he. It is clearly absurd that somebody can actually, two-thirds of the way, get an operation right and still be judged to be a failure – since E's and D's are counted and regarded as 'failures'.

For these and other reasons, normative assessments
are gravely suspect. But - and this is critical in
the Arts - the final criticism in this particular
case, that is fatally debilitating to this kind of
assessment, is this. The nature of the art object is
such that it is <u>ex-hypothesi individual</u>. Each work
of art has its own criteria of correctness and appro-
priateness and excellence within it, as judged proper
to it by the criteria of the person creating or per-
forming it. An individual artist has produced this
work, and it is not comparable against other people's
work in this - or any other - way. It has to be
looked at <u>per se</u> and <u>in se</u>, on its own terms, in its
own light and according to criteria of its own excellence. And to think, as normative assessors do, that
these things - works of Art - can be in any way <u>com-
pared</u> is to make a crucial and fatal category mistake.

There is one final point. Normative assessments
start from the premise that all people who take the
examinations or who are assessed at any one time
relative to each other are at the same point in their
individual development as regards their subject.
Suppose, for example, that I change schools and find
myself in my first term of Latin, having just been
put in from some other school where they never did
Latin before, suddenly being set a test which is,
frankly, beyond me, but alongside other pupils, some
of whom may have been doing Latin for one or two
years already. Clearly I shall fail relative to
them, even if my own progress may have been start-
ling. What happens in the case of normative assessments is the comparison of individuals who are in
radically different stages of development, <u>relative
to each other</u>. The error lies in assessors assuming
that test candidates are in some way the same. So
that the individual growth rate is also negated by
normative assessment.

In my view, then, in order to eliminate such dis-
functions, criterial assessments are obviously superior - though even they must be tempered with
judgments from each particular subject or <u>genre</u>,

applied on an individualistic basis. It is here that
consideration has to be given to the question of individual differences between learners and the necessity of adverting to differences in an individual's
rate and stage of development in a subject, so that
even criterial judgments can be modified in the light
of such knowledge as assessors might obtain from such
sources.

I wish to change the prevailing tenor of and approach
to the question of assessments in the Arts and in educational establishments, and to try to suggest a set
of principles for making criterial, individualistic
assessments in the worlds of the arts. I believe
that we ought to remember the following things that
will be fundamental to the making of such assessments.

First of all we must have a clear grasp of the logic
of aesthetic judgments: that aesthetic objects are
unique particularities within a specific genre, and
have to be looked at as such.

Secondly, that works of art are, as Louis Arnaud Reid
(1969) calls them, "embodiments" of whole layers and
textures of meaning, such that any attempt to differentiate between the various kinds and layers of meaning is to risk discomposing the unique particularity
that is the work of art. What we have to remember,
rather, is that particular feature of our appraisals
of art objects that Anton Ehrenzweig (1967) called
the 'de-differentiatedness' in our understanding of
the meanings of works of art. Thirdly, however, we
should remember that works of art are quite objective and thus that the making of objective judgments
with respect to them is perfectly possible. I say
that for this reason: the testing of the temperature
of water by a Centigrade thermometer is clearly a
model of objectivity - that of the scientific world.
But the scientific is not the only model of objectivity. Any intentional actions, such as signing a
cheque or standing in front of a man dressed in white
holding hands with a person of the opposite sex, are
objectifiable actions, that are amenable to appraisals that are quite as objective, in their own way, as
are scientific judgments (Best, 1978).

Thus, in our rendering objective our assessments in
and of the Arts, we have to remember the language -
the grammar and the syntax - that permits communication and constitutes objectivity in each particular
artistic genre. None who has heard of dancers, for
example, talking about the "language" of dance and
observed the ways in which they try to introduce
their students into its vocabulary will disagree that
each particular mode of discourse in the world of the
Arts has its own language (cf Hirst, 1965). Not only
that: each sub-world in the Arts has its own "literature". Some knowledge of the relevant literature of
the dance, art, sculpture and music is clearly important in forming and applying our judgments. As an
example, let us look at the judgments we make of
Dutch paintings of the 16th - 17th century, for instance. Here seems to be an area of the activity of
making artistic appraisals, in which not only must we
be able to speak some of the language; we must also,
I think, know some of the literature (cf Oakeshott,
1962; 1966).

As a fourth principle, I should like to suggest that
there is a crucial need for clarity about the judgmental nature of our assessment in the arts. We are
not making factual judgments in our assessments in
and of the Arts; we are not making empirical judgments in the arts about what is. We are not making
'summative' judgments, in other words, we are making
formative and evaluative ones - judgments that, by
being articulated, are going, in some way, to contribute to the process and furtherance of dialogue between individuals, set up by the publication or exhibition of the work of art itself.

Fifthly: we also have to be clear about the kinds of
achievements being looked for and the kinds of criteria and paradigms being employed in assessment. We
have to be willing to specify the kinds of information relevant to making informed judgments of the
work of art that we are perceiving and trying to
appreciate. We have to make decisions as to the optimum and the appropriate means of determining upon
and gathering this information, as to how best to report the findings. We must also have an awareness of
the uses to which our assessment will be put, for

assessment must and will take place, of and by individuals in a particular socio-historical context and
for particular socio-historical purposes.

Sixth: we should have the courage to stand up against
and refute the ignorant and the uninformed judgments
that some people make about the works and creations
of practitioners whose gifts and education make them
'authorities' in our fields. But, seventh, we must
not permit informed people to make judgments and
assessments in forms and by criteria that are, in the
view of such authorities, inappropriate, partial or
incoherent.

Assessments in the arts are different from assessments in other kinds of human activity, in other
modes of discourse, in the words and worlds of other
communities of scholars. They have not to be dis-
secting, discomposing or analytic; they have to be
synthesizing, de-differentiating, in a word, holistic.
And why that is has to do with the particular nature
of the art works; for these are created - and can
only be properly assessed - by those who are, in some
sense, what some people have called 'connoisseurs'
(Eisner, 1978). I am not talking here about 'high'
art or 'high' culture; I am talking about the application of criteria that originate in and rest on an
appropriate cognitive repertoire in the field. It is
perfectly possible to make intelligent, informed and
coherent aesthetic judgments of the musical creations
and contributions of Pink Floyd and Led Zepplin, as
it is of Brahms, Bach and Beethoven. The same point
will also be valid in the case of art, sculpture,
poetry and all the rest.

For my eighth principle I wish to return to my notion of the 'polyphony' of the arts - indeed a polyphony that is sometimes even a cacophony. For there
appears, very often, to be no point of contact in
common between disputants as to the "real meaning"
of a work of art. There is as much controversy as
to what constitutes "getting it right" in the world
of the arts, as there is in religion or morals or,
come to that, the world of science. But "getting it
right" in the arts is different and so problematic
because in our assessments of whether an artist has

D. Aspin

done that, we may work with different criteria, in different contexts, from different people with different intentions. And all these have to do with the logics that constitute aesthetic judgments.

Arts education in this respect, and assessment in the arts is, therefore, a paradigm of what W.B. Gallie (1955; 1956) called 'essential contestedness'. It is not possible, in the Arts, to make right or wrong judgments; the only thing that is possible is to be prepared to "take one's coat off", so to speak, and get down to an argument. "This is a poor picture", we might say, "Isn't it?" No, it isn't. It's absolutely marvellous". "Oh? Why is it?" And at that point argument, and the making of valid and informed assessments and judgments begins.

I am not one of those who meet such assessments with the response that "Well, that is, of course, only a value judgment", as though that marked the end of discourse. That would be to lend credence to a species of emotivism and subjectivism in aesthetics that I find profoundly implausible; indeed, it is, in my view, incoherent. There is, I believe, a real point in saying, "Yes, it is a value judgment". Because it is at that point that argument about the meaning, value and justification of our value judgments begins.

The kind of argument that I have in mind here is that kind which Karl Popper (1943; 1974) apotheosized as constituting the paradigm of an 'open' society: proposition/opposition; thesis/antithesis; conjecture/refutation. And the conjectures and refutations that are attempted in the arts are, in a quite definite sense, a model of that kind of community apotheosized by Popper as the 'open' society. In this connection, I have to say that I find Thomas Kuhn's (1970) thesis of 'relativistic' discontinuous paradigms, both in science and (as some have done) in the Arts, unconvincing. I maintain the open society has an objectivity that is based upon and concerned with the search for truth – in all its various forms. But not truth in the sense of the hard realities of mathematics or the empirical sciences only: the world we inhabit is a totality of all the various kinds of communicable meaningfulness, of a diverse

and variegated character, with regard to the objects
that all its constituent members produce for consumption, contemplation and satisfaction. In this sense,
and in this way, in the world of the Arts too, the
ultimate aim of all our assessments and judgment-
making is the pursuit of the Truth, the various versions of which make communication at all possible
within it, serve to define its limits and to adum-
brate the outlines of future developments of,
creations within and extensions to this world that we
share and value so highly.

For we too, share a common language that enables us
to say to each other (as Victor Hugo was once supposed to have said) "I disagree absolutely with what
you say, but I will fight to the death to defend your
right to say it." For it is because people can say
things to each other in our world, that it becomes
necessary and indeed important to us to attempt to
assess the values of what is said.

REFERENCES

Archambault, R.D. (ed), (1965). _Philosophical Analysis and Education._ Routledge and Kegan Paul.

Aspin, D.N., (1980). _The Arts, Education and the
Community._ Inaugural Lecture, 18th November 1980
King's College in the University of London.

Ayer, A.J., (1936). _Language, Truth and Logic._
Hutchinson.

Barrett, C. (ed), (1965). _Collected Essays in Aes-
thetics._ Basil Blackwell.

Best, D., (1978). _Philosophy and Human Movement._
Allen and Unwin.

Callaghan, J., Speech at Ruskin College on 18th October 1976 reported in the _Labour Weekly_ of 22nd
October 1976.

D. Aspin

DES., (1980). A Framework for the School Curriculum. H.M.S.O.

DES., (1979). Aspects of Secondary Education in England: A Survey by H.M. Inspectors of Schools. H.M.S.O.

DES., (1980). A View of the Curriculum. DES Series Matters for Discussion II. H.M.S.O.

DES., (1977). Curriculum 11-16. Working Papers by H.M. Inspectorate - A contribution to Current Debate; DES Information Division; Supplement June, 1979.

DES., (1977). Education in Schools: A Consultative Document (Green Paper). H.M.S.O. Cmnd 6869.

DES., (1979). Local Authority Arrangements for the School Curriculum. DES Review Circular 14/77. H.M.S.O.

Ehrenzweig, A., (1967). The Hidden Order of Art - A Study in the Psychology of Artistic Imagination. Weidenfeld and Nicholson.

Eisner, E.W., (1978). "On the uses of educational connoisseurship and criticism for evaluating classroom life" in Teachers College Record, 78/3, pp 345-358

Elton, W. (ed)., (1954). Aesthetics and Language. Blackwell.

Gallie, W.B., "Essentially Contested Concepts" in Proceedings of the Aristotelian Society, 1955-56.

Gallie, W.B., (1956). "Art as an Esseentially Contested Concept" in Philosophical Quarterly, Vol.6.

Greger, S., "Aesthetic Meaning" in Proceedings of the Philosophy of Education Society. July 1972, Vol. VI, No.2.

Hampshire, S., "Logic and Appreciation" in Elton (1954).

Hirst, P.H., and Peters, R.S., (1970). The Logic of Education. Routledge and Kegan Paul.

Hirst, P.H., (1973). Knowledge and the Curriculum. Routledge and Kegan Paul.

Hume, D. Treatise on Human Nature (Books II and III) and An Enquiry Concerning the Principles of Morals.

Kennick, W.E., "Does Traditional Aesthetics Rest on a Mistake?" in Barrett, C., (1965).

Kuhn, T.S., (1970). The Structure of Scientific Revolutions. University of Chicago Press (2nd edition).

Najder, Z., (1975). Values and Evaluation. Clarendon Press.

Oakeshott, M., (1962). Rationalism in Politics and Other Essays. Methuen.

Oakeshott, M., (1966). Experience and its Modes. Cambridge University Press.

Peters, R.S., (1966). Ethics and Education. Allen and Unwin.

Peters, R.S., (1973). Authority, Responsibility and Education. Allen and Unwin.

Pitcher, G., (ed), (1969). Wittgenstein. Macmillan.

Popper, K.R., (1943). The Open Society and its Enemies. Vols. I and II. Routledge and Kegan Paul.

Popper, K.R., (1972). Objective Knowledge. Clarendon Press.

Popper, K.R., (1974). Conjectures and Refutations. Routledge and Kegan Paul.

Reid, L. Arnaud., (1957). "The Philosophy of Education Through the Arts" in the Report of the

<u>Conference</u> of the Joint Council for Education
Through Art in the Royal Festival Hall, London,
April 1957: <u>A Consideration of Humanity, Technol-</u>
<u>ogy and Education in our Time.</u>

Reid, L. Arnaud., (1969). <u>Meaning in the Arts</u>.
Allen and Unwin.

Ross, M., (1980). <u>Hard Core: The Predicament of the</u>
<u>Arts</u> in Aspects, Vol. 2. University of Exeter,
School of Education.

Sockett, H., (ed), (1980). <u>Accountability in the Eng-</u>
<u>lish Education System</u>. Hodder and Stoughton.

Stevenson, C.L., (1943). <u>Ethics and Language</u>. Yale
University Press.

Stevenson, C.L., (1963). <u>Facts and Values</u>. Yale
University Press.

Straughan, R., and Wrigley, J., (eds), (1980).
<u>Values and Evaluation in Education</u>. Harper and
Row.

Strawson, P.F., (1974). "Aesthetic Appraisal and
Works of Art" in his <u>Freedom and Resentment and</u>
Other Essays. Methuen.

Waismann, F., (edited by Harre, R.,)(1965). <u>The</u>
<u>Principles of Linguistic Philosophy</u>. Macmillan.

Wittgenstein, L., (1953). <u>Philosophical Investiga-</u>
<u>gations</u> (trans. Anscombe, G.E.M.,). Basil Black-
well.

Wittgenstein, L., (1966). <u>Lectures and Conversations</u>
<u>on Aesthetics, Psychology and Religious Belief</u>
edited by Barret, C. Basil Blackwell.

The Assessment of Aesthetic
Development in the Visual Mode

ERNEST GOODMAN

I don't think that I've had such an alarming lack of
self-confidence in tackling an assignment since my
C.O., at one point during my picaresque career in the
army said to me "You've done a course in Pay and
Accounting, haven't you? Right, I'm putting you in
charge of mechanical and electrical equipment on
Monday."

Malcolm Ross will confirm that my first response to
his invitation to speak on this subject was to refuse. Having done so, however, I turned to a kind of
guilt-ridden pondering as to the reasons for my refusal. Swiftly acknowledging basic incompetence and
cowardice took little time ... but further thought
revealed other problems. The first was that so far
very little is known about either aesthetic development or its assessment and little work has been done
in this field - presumably because those with the
time, opportunity and resources have always thought
that they had other, weightier fish to fry and that
the aesthetic dimension was a kind of 'tiddler' for
which the only appropriate action was to throw it
back. Allied to this is the fact that the structures
and methods of assessment and evaluation of general
use and respectability have always been largely inappropriate and inadequate in relation to the aesthetic field.

Even in non-aesthetic areas, such methods have recently come under severe questioning and alternatives
sought. Malcolm Parlett (1974), a disciple of what
he calls 'illuminative evaluation' has this to say

about them:-

> " ..... results from such studies rarely
> carry conviction: they present an ema-
> ciated and artificial picture of real-
> world educational life. The results
> are usually numerical in form and dif-
> ficult to mesh with the 'qualitative'
> view of the world held by most of us ..
> ... this basic experimental model I have
> referred to elsewhere as the 'agricult-
> ural/botany paradigm: appropriate for
> testing fertilisers on carefully tended
> fields of crops at agricultural re-
> search stations, but inappropriate and
> incongruous for monitoring how inno-
> vations become absorbed and adapted in
> a diversity of school settings, by
> teachers with different perspectives,
> teaching separate and distinctive
> groups of children."

Among Parlett's requirements for an alternative model
are that it should be applicable to situations as
they actually exist - also that it should lead to
studies that are useful and interesting. As he says
"What is the good of research reports that are never
read?" This seems to me to be good, meaty, common-
sense stuff - a world away from the standard devia-
tions and so forth of orthodox evaluation - apart
from other forms of deviation - like cooking the figures!

Large scale empirical and statistical methods were
originally imported from science in order to give
status to the then newly developing education departments. But it is as well from the beginning to remember that education is an art - not a science - and
that there are few educational certainties. I can
think of three: -

> 1. That if you don't teach something,
> many of your pupils won't learn it ...
> furthermore that most of your pupils
> will assume that it's not worth learn-
> ing. The others won't think about it.

2. That even if you do teach it, a
number of your pupils won't learn it.

3. That among those who display indi-
cations of learning it, there will be
some who are instead learning other
things of which you are unaware.

Among the functions of assessment are to reveal things
which are not taught which might with benefit be
taught .... and to reveal the incidence both of non-
learning and 'unintended' learning.

I have also found myself, as a former art teacher,
sharing the largely intuitive misgivings of art
teachers in general about measurement, perhaps because of a healthy suspicion that what has so far
passed for assessment and evaluation generally in education has been a kind of private, esoteric game for
members of education departments, with the prize of
doctorates for the winners .... more than a suspicion
also that such people usually attempt only to assess
those aspects of education which seem to lend themselves easily to precise measurement, and that other
aspects become victims of what might be called the
'disappearance by default' syndrome - (the notion
that what can't be measured doesn't exist) - and van-
ish in a kind of educational 'Bermuda Triangle' !

Teachers fear, therefore, that even if conventional
methods were applied to art this would fragment and
distort the art experience. This fear is sometimes
expanded to cover any form of assessment. Elliot
Eisner (1972) describes these fears well in a paper
called 'The Mythology of Art Education'. He writes:-

> "This belief is .... that art is an in-
> dividual and personal thing. It should
> not be evaluated by someone other than
> its creator. The argument proceeds
> that the imposition of external cri-
> teria and standards are not only in-
> appropriate to the nature of artistic
> activity but that they generate
> anxiety in children that blocks the
> pathways that must remain open for

creativity to result .... Isn't this
one of the few places in the entire
curriculum where children should feel
unfettered, free of artificial and conventional standards and rules? What is
being sought in art is a personal and
authentic individuality, not the pro-
production of predetermined forms to be
measured and graded like eggs or cheese.

Now I think that the fact that the
people who argue that children's art
should not be evaluated are among the
first to exclaim their outrage when
they see work that they consider 'tight'
doesn't seem to pose a problem for them.
The fact is that evaluation, even for
those who claim not to do it, is being
done all the time .... I go even further in saying that not to evaluate
children's art (even if this were possible, which I don't think it is) is to
be educationally irresponsible. Education is a goal-directed activity as
teachers are concerned not simply with
bringing about change, but with bringing
about desirable change. If the teacher
does not evaluate what children do, how
can he determine if what he is doing is
contributing to or hampering their
growth in art? If you don't evaluate as
a teacher, how do you know if you are
helping or hurting the kids, and on what
basis?

Of course imposition, interference and
insensitive appraisal can hamper the
child's development in art, but anything
can be done badly .... in addition, the
constant approval of what the children
produce regardless of its quality or the
effort that went into the work may back-
fire .... children respect thoughtful
evaluation because it testifies to them
that their teachers are taking their
work seriously."

When I taught art I used to feel that after a long
training I was fully capable of assessing my pupils'
work in a rapid, holistic, no-nonsense, unstructured
way, and that this, together with the checks and bal-
ances of the external examination system and a reasonably well thought out syllabus were all that one
could reasonably ask. There is no doubt that this
view was influenced, whether consciously or not, by
the meagre allocation of time to my subject and the
heavy demands on the extra-curricular time of a con-
scientious art teacher. These problems are still
real ones and while I believe that there are a number
of good reasons why we should commit ourselves to
more serious and systematic attention to assessment,
there is a responsibility upon those who wish to help
teachers to be realistic - and not, in their enthusiasm, to seek to promote systems which most teachers
would find too difficult to sustain.

Against this background then I finally decided that
so far in the world of assessment there have been too
many chiefs and too few Indians - also that witch-
doctors have had rather too much influence. It seems
to me that if the views of honest and well-meaning
labourers in our field had been expressed and taken
account of at the appropriate time some, at least, of
the larger lunacies of educational assessment might
have been avoided. It is on this basis that I share
with you my tentative thoughts and speculations about
assessment and consent to display my uncertainties.
It is also why I am sure that art teachers have to
overcome their traditional dislike of formal assessment and enter into sustained enquiry and dialogue on
how we can all become more effective in recognising
and assessing the aesthetic development of pupils -
its success and deficiencies - not only for the benefit of the pupils themselves but also as a check on
our own effectiveness.

This has always been desirable, but I would suggest
that a new urgency has now developed for two main
reasons:-

        1. Because of greater recent emphasis
        upon teacher accountability. This is
        likely to mean ultimately that if you

don't find satisfactory ways of evaluating the outcomes of what you teach,
someone else is likely to do it for you
- and in so doing possibly to redefine
your role. There is no guarantee in
that case that the criteria used would
be such as you would find acceptable.

2. Because you tend to gain rather
than lose in the current struggle for a
place in the curriculum sun by making
public, in a coherent way, the criteria
and values which are usually at the
moment only implicit in your judgements
of children's work. The respect accorded to visual aesthetic education is
likely to be enhanced if this is done,
and the implications of this for its
position in the curriculum are surely
clear. If, however, we prefer that our
practice remain undisclosed and apparently esoteric, we cannot then complain if
we and our work are viewed with the distanced suspicion usually accorded to
medicine men and their rituals, and, in
a harsh world of shrinking schools and
curricula, regarded as a costly luxury.

I think, perhaps, that I should now pause for a moment to ensure that there is no confusion about my
use of terms. Strictly speaking, 'assessment' merely
means the collection of information - of levels of
competence or whatever. 'Evaluation' signifies the
applying of values to the process. These two in
practice tend to overlap and enmesh. For instance,
we apply values even at the stage of choosing what to
attempt to assess.

There is another word which I may use from time to
time - 'monitoring'. This signifies the making of
repeated, periodic assessments from which to identify
movement - as for instance improvement or weakening
in specific areas, or changing patterns of priorities.
In passing may I just note that the term 'development'
in the title of this talk does imply a form of monitoring, and this means that the end-on external

examination is, apart from other reasons, inappropriate for this purpose.

This brings me rationally to the different forms of
assessment and the different purposes they serve.   I
shall consider three .... and two of these very
briefly. The three are national assessment and monitoring, as in the case of the APU., LEA forms of
these, and in-school assessment.

I shall not spend much time upon the APU separately -
not only because I understand that it has already
been dealt with in this series, but because there are
more pressing issues for teachers in connection with
their in-school assessments. They should, however,
make themselves aware of what is happening in the APU,
both because its work could, ultimately, furnish them
with useful assessment instruments, and because it
could, if things go wrong, exert influences of a possibly undesirable kind. So far, as you know, the APU
study of the aesthetic field is still exploratory and
no decisions have yet been made about national or any
other kind of assessment in this field. As for LEA
exercises, I am sure that other speakers present today will know a great deal more than I do about
these.

However, it is crucial to note that both the APU and
LEA modes are essentially different from in-school
assessment. Both are distanced from actual children.
The APU seeks means of gathering accurate information
about the general level of attainment in various
areas of the curriculum and to monitor periodically.
It is then intended that the information so gained
will be evaluated by those responsible for educational policy, with particular reference to the allocation
of resources and in-service training. No information
about particular children or schools will be made
available by this mode. In theory LEA exercises will
be of a similar character on a smaller scale, gathering information about levels of attainment across the
LEA. Bearing in mind, however, the relative autonomy
of LEAs, there seems to be little doubt that their
schemes will vary widely and that in some cases they
will have as a major objective the comparative testing of schools.

As with other aspects of curriculum development, however, it is my belief that the real hope for any significant progress in assessment lies with teachers in
schools, acting both individually and, as I shall
stress later, in groups. Teachers are in constant
touch with the realities of the educational process,
can operate assessment, evaluation and monitoring as
diagnostic tools for the benefit of actual children
whom they know, and - something of much importance -
they can do this as an integral part of a continuous
teaching process, not as brief, detached interventions
as in the case of external assessments or examinations.
Because of their close and continuing experience of
the ways in which particular children or groups of
children respond to the various aspects of the educational encounter they can provide valuable insights
not only for the refinement of their own practice
but for the guidance of those outside schools who engage in the design of assessment models and instruments. No-one can surely now deny the importance of
art teachers improving their own practice so that
they are in a position to check and steer externally
developed systems.

So I shall now concentrate on the in-school assessment of the aesthetic development of children in the
visual mode - that is looking in an informed, sensitive and appropriately focussed way at the qualitative perceptions and judgements children make about
visual forms, symbols and images in relation to their
own work, to that of others, and to the natural world
.... with the twin aims of helping children to grow
aesthetically and of refining the teaching process
which seeks to accomplish this. More of this later.

At this point a word of caution is necessary. Having
implied, if not stated, that there now needs to occur
some shift of emphasis from what might be called the
initiating aspects of teaching to the evaluation of
what has been initiated, it is nevertheless absolutely
crucial to remember that the two are closely related.
It is perhaps obvious that there is rarely much point
in attempting to assess something which hasn't been
taught .... but it seems to be far less obvious that
there is also little point in assessing something
which should not have been taught in the first place.

In other words, the <u>whole</u> package must be reasonably
sensible before any worthwhile evaluation can be done.
Put in another way, if forced to make the choice, I
would always choose the sensitive, energetic teacher
whose general aims and methods were sensible and well
thought through who was not good at assessment rather
than the assessment expert who couldn't get anything
else right. It is amazing how often teachers still
attempt to assess children not only by means of crude
and reductionist instruments such as those which
measure memory when purporting to measure intelligence but on the basis of ill-chosen and insensitive-
ly administered tasks. One of the most horrific examples I know of this is recounted by Charles Silberman (1973) in his book 'Crisis in the Classroom'. He
tells of a visit to a school in these words:

> "The students in a sixth-grade English
> class in a school on a Chippewa Indian
> reservation are all busily at work,
> writing a composition for Thanksgiving.
> The subject of the composition is writ-
> ten on the blackboard for the students
> (and the visitor) to see. It is "Why
> we are Happy the Pilgrims Came"!"

This is an extreme case, but it does reveal a dimension of in-school evaluation which does not apply in
external modes. This could be called 'Subject-
Qualified Evaluation', implying that the tasks upon
which evaluation is based as well as the character of
the evaluation itself have to take into account not
just the age, but as far as possible also the back-
grounds, interests and so forth of the pupils concerned. I cannot, for instance, conceive of any worthwhile English flowing from most of the classes I
taught in Manchester if set tasks similar to that
suffered by the Indian children.

There is another condition which has to be guarded
against and to which evaluators are particularly
prone, as are many Headteachers. This is the condition of instant readiness to be seduced by systems.
A victim of this becomes intoxicated when confronted
by a system of sufficient sophistication and
complexity.   The symptoms of the

condition in the assessment field are manifest when
the importance and relevance of the thing assessed
are subordinate to its suitability for processing by
the system. A prime case of this which I saw fairly
recently was a major item in the art assessments of
the American NAEP programme (National Assessment of
Educational Progress). This consisted of asking
children to draw a man running. Scores of objective
ways were then developed to assess the resulting
drawings, including such things as how many arms and/
or legs were shown. I also recall that marks were
assigned for introducing lines symbolising speed - as
in children's comics. All the results were, of
course, quantified and analysed by computer. I leave
it to you to speculate as to how much this would contribute to a national assessment of the levels of artistic achievement by young people - but the point I
wish to make is that the fact that the exercise set
is one which rarely forms part of any sensible art
course in the first place seems either to have es-
caped everybody's attention or to have been forced
out of their consciousness by fascination with the
system.

Let us, therefore, seek sensible procedures which
teachers can operate and control, which will enable
us to look more searchingly and revealingly at what
we are actually doing to the children whom we teach,
making sure at the same time that what we do does not
trivialise the whole process. Let us also guard
against a finicky preoccupation with relatively un-
important minutiae, but seek instead to build up for
each of our pupils a full profile of aesthetic
achievement and development in terms of their visual
experience. Apart from the uses already mentioned
this seems to me to be a necessary prerequisite to
discussing with any authority the aesthetic growth of
children with parents and Headteachers. It is also a
testimony to our professionalism.

Let us be clear as to what we are considering. Aesthetic competence is built basically upon perceptions
through the senses - in our case the visual sense.
These perceptions will be simple or complex, confused
or clear according to such things as the sensitivity
of the perceptual apparatus, and the store of what

Edmund Feldman (1967) calls 'funded perception'.
Aesthetic perceptions focus upon the qualitative and
symbolic aspects of the forms of our world, rather
than their logic or 'practical' significance ....
much as a child forgets the capacity to soak through
his leaky shoes of the water in a puddle into which
he has stepped, in his delight in its changing visual
forms. So a good art teacher will take care in various ways to exercise and sensitise the visual senses
of his pupils and constantly to enrich their store of
visual aesthetic experience.

Aesthetic perceptions can be enjoyed sensuously for
their own sake .... and the world would be a poor and
dull place indeed if this were not possible. Some
believe this capacity to be a biological necessity.
But they are also harnessed in more complex ways to
enrich our knowledge and understanding not only of
the objective world, but also of our inner worlds,
since a major property of aesthetic experience is
that it engages our feelings and furnishes us with
means to explore and express them (Witkin, 1974).

When perceptions are harnessed in aesthetic action
this takes fundamentally two forms - making compositions of forms or images on the one hand, and appraising them on the other. Again, both are enmeshed in a
sound course; the making of an artifact by a child
should involve constant aesthetic appraisal, judgement and readjustment, and the aesthetic judgements
made about the work of others should be made deeper
and more insightful by the process of creating. Both
these modes of aesthetic operation, therefore, need
to be assessed if a rounded picture of aesthetic
achievement is to be built up. It has to be remem-
bered that some aesthetic experience and insights
cannot emerge solely through the practical work of
the child, just as aesthetic judgements based too exclusively upon the appraisal of the work of others
are likely to lack the personal commitment and conviction which can result from experience of the creative act from the inside (Wilson, 1980). At the
same time we have also to expect that some children
will display a greater range of sensitivity and personal judgement in appraising work other than their
own than they can reveal in their own efforts .... as

in the case of children who have difficulty with the
control of media.

It is again necessary to pause here to clarify certain issues. Firstly, when I speak of 'appraising'
the work of others I do not mean 'history of art', in
the sense of placing works in their historical period
or style, detecting the artist, and remembering details of his private life and the milieu in which he
operated. This may be very useful to historians and
sociologists, but such knowledge is essentially 'non-
aesthetic' and of itself gives no evidence whatsoever
of aesthetic sensitivity. It may, in its broader implications, have a place with other elements in helping to evaluate artefacts in context, but a great
deal more enquiry needs to take place in this field.

The second point I want to make is that when I use
the term 'the work of others' I do not have in mind
only the more traditional, major fine art forms, but
would include virtually all man-made objects, dis-
positions of forms and imagery which possess aesthetic potential .... that is the capacity to attract
aesthetic attention, arouse aesthetic response or
give aesthetic satisfaction. This is, of course, a
vast field, from which each teacher has to make intelligent and appropriate selections, and it includes
the contemporary as well as the traditional, the
ephemeral as well as the lasting, the humble as well
as the noble, the common as well as the exotic, the
vulgar as well as the refined, ... and all these
made manifest through dress, personal adornment, electronic media, commercial and social graphics, toys,
buildings, ritual, environmental design and so forth.
If aesthetic competencies are firmly established and
robust they can be applied to virtually the whole of
our visual experience and if they are to remain robust, they should be so applied. Put in another way,
I would claim that a major intention of aesthetic education is to make available the option, and develop
the habit, of regarding the whole of the world aesthetically, not to provide a kind of mental pocket of
values and criteria which is only switched on when
entering an art gallery or a cathedral.

I make these points because their exists a very

influential school of thought in the field of aesthetic education which relates it firmly to 'high'
culture and which seems to view the practical efforts
of children as largely emotional therapy and, therefore, irrelevant to the process. Here is a recent
statement by a leading member of this school:-

> "I think the primary purpose of aesthetic
> education is to provide pupils with the
> skills, knowledge and disposition for
> the cultivated enjoyment of works of
> art. We want pupils not only to be able
> to enjoy, but also to discuss and judge
> works of art with the sensibility and
> categories of the educated person.
> (Smith, 1978)."

This view is associated with the idea that as the accepted noble works of fine art have the highest levels of complexity and quality, they are the most
suitable medium for aesthetic education.

The truth of the matter is, in my view, that this is
one of the possible purposes of aesthetic education
and may be achieved in a small number of cases in our
school system. It is, however, a selective aim and
is very difficult indeed to relate to the majority of
the children whom I have taught or whose education I
have organised - children who, in general, will rarely if ever visit an art gallery again when they leave
school but who will have to make judgements for the
rest of their lives about their dress, the image they
present to others, the small environments they create
in and around their homes, the aesthetic quality of
the objects with which they surround themselves, and
the way they respond to the multitude of visual images which confront their consciousness throughout
their waking hours.

As far as assessment is concerned, I suggest that we
may find out more about, for instance, a girl's levels of aesthetic perception and judgement by looking
sensitively and searchingly at the images of the
world which she creates and by the judgements she
makes of the visual quality of the things which are
close or dear to her than by asking for her responses

to a coloured photograph of the ceiling of the
Sistine Chapel .... although I should add that this
doesn't mean that we shouldn't try to find out from
time to time what children make of such works, particularly where we have good reasons for associating
them with the actual aesthetic problems which the
children tackle in their practical work.

Incidentally, while writing the reference to the
Sistine Chapel, a bizarre image came into my mind of
one of the classes I have known, with a high proportion of children from families of West Indian ori-
gin, obediently settling to write an essay entitled
"Why we are glad about the High Renaissance" !

I have said that aesthetic competence is built upon
repeated aesthetic perceptions derived from and applied to different situations. Let us be clear, however, that aesthetic competence does not develop entirely separately from other forms of competence or
consciousness (Ornstein, 1974) - its development is
aided by non-aesthetic competences and experiences,
like control of media, knowledge of processes and vocabulary, knowledge of the broad categories of artefacts, the contexts in which they are produced, and
so on. Judged in isolation, these can give no direct
indication of levels of aesthetic operation, but they
are enabling agents in its development and we, therefore, need to look at how they operate in the context
of aesthetic acts. Also, because they need to be
attended to in the teaching process, we need to assess
whether children are making progress in these areas
or not.

Flexibility of response to aesthetic problems in
practical work cannot emerge strongly unless children
have explored the possibilities of the media they are
using and gained adequate control of a range of such
possibilities. The pencil is a fine and sensitive
tool for the making of expressive statements only
when a wide range of its marks can be exploited.

But our central task in assessing aesthetic competence and development involves looking at the different kinds and levels of children's visual perceptions so let us now focus in more sharply on these. My view is that they are basically of four main kinds:- At the simplest level there is recognition-of what is being attended to. Properly speaking, this level cannot be confidently classified as aesthetic in character, though there is some academic argument about this. Recognition of this kind may need few or many visual 'clues', and the creation of a full image from an incomplete set of clues is part of the complex mechanism of aesthetic operation. This aspect, therefore, at least merits attention.

There will be no argument from art teachers about the necessity of attention to the second level - that of formal qualities such as tone or colour, the capacity to attend to them singly and to recognise graduations of intensity, size or whatever. Advanced perceptions at this level would include such things as sensitive perception of the relative tone values of coloured or textured areas.

At the third level perceptions of relationships of aesthetic forms are involved - both within a single element and between elements, and these will vary from simple to complex. Here, therefore, we enter the realm of the structural systems of artefacts - perception of how they are built and such things as what conventions are used to represent three-dimensional reality in two dimensions. Degrees of coherence in simple or complex formal arrangements are perceived and at advanced level structural frameworks are discerned in spite of a mass of confusing detail. The ability to categorise structural systems is also based on such perceptions.

At the heart of the aesthetic perception, however, is the recognition and use of forms, formal qualities and structural systems for expressive purposes - to create atmosphere, mood or character and to convey feeling and meaning. This is a highly sophisticated level of aesthetic achievement and must be recognised and prized as such (Reid, 1969).

AI - F

As with other forms of development, some children
reach higher levels than others at school and the
various levels are reached more quickly by some than
others. Gifted children seem to move swiftly at an
early age to familiarity with structural systems and
even to the level of fluent use of the expressive
mode (Goodman, 1977). My view is that one of the important functions of assessment is to reveal at what
stage particular pupils are operating so that teaching may take account of this.

I would not attempt in a lecture of this kind to deal
in any detail with methods of assessment, since much
of what I would say would be highly speculative.
There is a pressing need for rigorous conceptual and
experimental work on this aspect - at all levesl of
the service, but particularly by teachers, for reasons
already mentioned. I shall suggest some general <u>pro-
cedures</u>, but would for the moment like to offer certain <u>principles</u> which might merit consideration.
These are:-

> 1.   That assessment and evaluation
> should be carried out with a well-thought
> out set of criteria, intentions and pro-
> cedures in mind.
>
> 2.   That they should as far as possible
> make use of sustained work done by pupils
> as part of a normal, sequentially develop-
> ing course.
>
> 3.   That an attempt should nevertheless
> be made to gain a rounded picture of vis-
> ual aesthetic competence and development
> of each pupil. This might mean that
> where the day to day work is such that
> particular aspects of aesthetic operation
> are not revealed, it may be necessary to
> devise and apply appropriate aesthetic
> problems for this purpose.

4. That ways be sought constantly to assess aesthetic skills non-verbally.

5. That in the appraisal of artefacts created by others, use should be made whenever possible of original objects and that pupils should not, in general, be required to express their judgements in sustained prose, since it is possible to possess visual aesthetic powers without possessing the necessary skills to express them in that way.

6. That care be taken not to allow assessment to become an end in itself or to warp the learning process.

It is likely that it will be found that no single method of assessment will suffice, but rather that a battery of instruments will be necessary. These could include critical appraisal by informed assessors - i.e. art teachers and others, short highly-specific practical tests, pencil and paper tests, multiple answer tests, 'jig-saw' type tests, recorded oral responses, photographed records of stages in the development of sustained work, pooled judgements, and so on.

When we move from the assessment of work at any given point to the consideration of development other dimensions emerge. There is a sense in which we are all, naturally, possessed of what might be called 'aesthetic drives'. J.Z. Young, the anatomist, has claimed that because of the way in which the brain is programmed we are all symbol-creating creatures and our searching for satisfying patterns is a biological function of humans. He sees art and artists as enriching and opening up to new experience this side of our nature (1978). However, experience suggests that without aesthetic education this drive can be relatively atrophied or turned into unprofitable byways and dead-ends where aesthetic sensitivity and imagination wither.

But if healthy development depends on education, we
need to be clear about what this entails - in other
words we need to identify what constitutes development and along what sort of lines it occurs. These
might be called the criteria of aesthetic development.
Here is interesting and challenging work indeed for
groups of teachers. On the basis of the outline
framework of aesthetic operation which I have already
sketched, may I just give a selection of examples
(not an exhaustive list) of possible lines of development in the visual mode:-

1. Control of Media

From
Clumsiness
Restricted range of mark-making
Marks unrelated to context

Etc.

To
Confident control
Wide range
Marks selected as appropriate to context

2. Perception

From
Limited and repetitive recall of visual forms
Coarse discrimination only of visual elements, eg tone, colour

Parts considered separately and inadequately related
Orthodox and predictable solutions to visual problems
Tendency constantly to resort to visual cliches
Only simple solutions produced
Visual elements used for identification and delimiting of forms only
Appraisal of artefacts at recognition and personal preference levels only
'Object-dominated' condition i.e. powers of imaginative recreation blocked by domination of naturalistic appearance of object.

To
Rich visual repertoire

Powers of fine discrimination
Perception and handling of more subtle graduations
Keen sense of structural coherence

Flexible, divergent operation

Experiment with personal solutions

Complex solutions sometimes appear
Expressive use of elements

Ability to appraise full aesthetic potential of a work

Free-ranging capacity for imagery using object as point of departure.

Serious, committed and sustained work on this vital
aspect would not only test the validity of concepts
such as these, but could fill out the range to the
point where a full profile of development could be
contemplated. Serious work also needs to be done not
just on the poles of these continua, but also on in-
termediate stages.

I am now near the end of my paper, but before I finish I feel I must give some tentative answers to a
question which must be at the back of the minds of
most teachers here - that is, assuming the good sense
of all this, how do we cope with all the work involved.
I can sympathise fully with this cri-de-coeur and
would first repeat that in extreme situations greater
precision in assessment would not be my first priority
for the improvement of art education. Nevertheless
it is important and justifies considerable help for
teachers from HMI, LEA advisers, education departments in higher education and other agencies. I
shall do my best personally to promote this view at
the Schools Council, the APU and H.M. Inspectorate,
and to engage the interest and energies of post-
graduate departments in this work.

But let us remember once more that good curriculum
development is what thoughtful teachers have found
possible and effective. What can be done, therefore,
in schools which would not impose impossible burdens?

The first thing, obviously, is that criteria have to
be sorted out, as I have suggested earlier. No full
and accurate assessment can be done until this has
been accomplished. Any teacher taking on GCE or CSE
marking has to accept this, and building a full profile of the aesthetic achievement of a child is much
more complex than examination marking. Then it would
be a major step forward for art education in this
country if every art department kept, for each child,
a folder of all his art work since entry into the
school. The work could be dated and, perhaps, filed
in categories - there is room for experiment here.

Without this, judgements about development must be, to a degree, suspect.

If this _is_ done, other worthwhile possibilities emerge. Not only can a child's work be assessed by the teacher responsible at any given time, but by all the art teachers in the school. This communal form of assessment not only offers the possibility of more reliable assessment, but is a valuable form of in-service training.

It need not, however, stop at teachers within the department - I have found it very valuable from time to time to bring into school experienced teachers or other art educationists from outside institutions to examine and comment upon the collected work of pupils - and to discuss it with them. Another idea worth pursuing is that of sinking one's pride and chauvinism and engaging in joint assessment exercises with the staffs of other schools.

The prospect of engaging children in this kind of exercise more than has been usual so far ought at least to be considered - the advantages of this are obvious and in some cases perhaps this kind of experience might do more for their aesthetic development than some other activities in which they engage.

And what about inviting interested and sensitive teachers from other departments to become involved? Once more the advantages are obvious, even if these do not all necessarily lie in the field of assessment.

It is, of course, _you_ who will decide what is possible in your particular situations. Whatever structure you develop, may I just suggest that some adequate, brief, manageable form of recording assessments needs to be found. This could take many forms, but things like the drawing up of profiles in graph form, or with the aid of five-point scales are among the systems which might be considered seriously in this context.

I wish you all well in this important work. Your energies will undoubtedly flag but let there be no doubt about the importance of anything which improves

the quality of the aesthetic education which children
experience, particularly in these desolate times. We
each create our own personal construct for reality
(Ornstein, 1974), and its richness and variety, and,
therefore, the capacity of the world to engage our
wonder, our imagination and our love, depend on the
aesthetic sensibility we are able to bring to its
contemplation. Without this, the world is indeed a
dull and a menacing thing. Logic alone is a thin
armour when the darkness moves in.

Harry Broudie put it well I think when he wrote:-

> "You don't get the news from poetry, but
> men die miserably every day for lack of
> what may be found there."

REFERENCES

Eisner, Elliot W., (1972), The Mythology of Art Edu-
    cation. Paper read to Department of Educational
    Studies, Brighton Polytechnic.

Eisner, Elliot W., (1979), The Educational Imagination.
    Collier Macmillan.

Feldman, Edmund B., (1967), Varieties of Visual
    Experience. Prentice Hall Inc.

Goodman, Ernest A., (1977), The Education of Children
    Gifted in the Visual Arts, in Trends in Education.
    HMSO.

Ornstein, Robert, (1974), The Psychology of Conscious-
    ness. W.H. Freeman.

Parlett, Malcolm, (1974), The New Evaluation, Trends
    in Education No. 34. HMSO.

Reid, Louis Arnaud, (1969), Meaning in the Arts.
    Allen and Unwin.

Silberman, Charles E., (1973), Crisis in the Class-
    room. Wildwood House.

Smith, Ralph A., (1978), <u>Some Notes on Educational</u>
<u>Evaluation, with Special Reference to Aesthetic</u>
<u>Education</u>. Paper read to members of the APU.

Wilson, Patrick, (1980), <u>Aesthetic Education and The</u>
<u>Compulsory Curriculum</u>, in The Journal of Curricu-
lum Studies, Vol. 12, No.1.

Witkin, Robert, (1974), <u>The Intelligence of Feeling</u>.
Heinemann.

Young, J.Z., (1978), <u>Programs of The Brain</u>, Oxford
University Press. (Particularly Chapter 20,
'Enjoying, Playing and Creating'.)

Some very unrealistic
ideas.

To Examine the Examination

BEN BRADNACK

There are a number of reasons for looking more
seriously than usual now at examinations in drama in
education.

There is, firstly, the historical expansion of public
examinations relevant to curriculum drama, which
started quite slowly with the development of 4th and
5th year drama options in the late 1960s, which led
to increasing CSE syllabuses in Modes 1 and 3. The
process accelerated with ROSLA, and the need which
developed from that to make courses attractive to
students stigmatised as 'non-academic' who had to be
persuaded that Drama, though lacking vocational
attraction, could secure them an additional 'qualification' if they worked at it. Drama moved there-
after into increasing competition in the traditional
'academic' educational sectors via the AEB and
London 'AO' and 'O' levels and evenutally arrived in
the strictly VIth form curriculum through CSE and
finally the fully fledged 'A' level in Theatre
Studies, now offered on the open market for the first
time by A.E.B. The Drama examination industry must
almost match micro-processing as the expansionist
wonder-boy in an industrial world otherwise
obstinately disinclined to expand. Such a perverse
phenomenon is, in itself, worth examining.

Moreover, the acceptance of the AEB 'A' level in
Theatre Studies by the Schools Council means that
this year a sort of continuity of public examinations
has at last been established in the field of Drama.
This means that Drama now has theoretical parity
with the rest of the established (i.e. examined)

curriculum.

This parity has, in a sense, been underwritten by the
abandonment of 'N' and 'F' last year; which really
means that 'A' levels, including Theatre Studies 'A'
level, are here to stay for the foreseeable future.
But whereas abandonment of 'N' and 'F' may constitute
for other subjects an invitation to inertia, for
drama, by contrast, it constitutes a challenge; for
the new 'A' level now has to struggle to rise to
'proper' as opposed to 'theoretical', 'A' level
status; it has to prove attractive not just to the
Schools Council who merely validate it, but to
students, to schools, to teachers and (the real test
of an 'A' level), to the 'consumers' of the 'product';
the institutions of higher education who have to
accept it as a qualification; and, to a lesser but
still significant extent, the employers. But at
least one University Admissions Board has given the
pilot syllabus, at any rate, a 'thumbs down'.
Amongst the concerns expressed by the assessors, which
were passed on to my own college in 1979, there appears an obsession with the 'qualifications' of the
practical examiners, and the 'standards' which they
will apply, subsumed in the hysterical tone of '.....
to recognise these proposals for matriculation purpose
would be suicidal'. These objections, and a difficulty with foreign texts (one assessor wishes for
less foreign texts, while another seems to imply
that English texts may merely duplicate English
literature syllabuses) are apparently inseparable
from the business of examinations, and they crucially
fail to respond to the possibility that a syllabus is
there primarily to be taught, and only much less
significantly to be examined. But the more significant point is that the university had the whip hand,
certainly for as long as the scheme remained experimental, to accept or reject as they chose; and if
they chose to reject for silly reasons, there seems
no way of rejecting their rejection: students were
not   able to use this 'A' level to gain admission
to this university.

But, since acceptance by the Schools Council of the
new 'A' level, the situation has again presumably become fluid - indeed, perhaps volatile. The arguments

raised by universities, and the volatility engendered
by their responses, constitute another reason to look
closely now at drama examinations.

A third and perhaps even more urgent reason to look
closely now at drama examinations, is the current
educational climate: the demand for 'accountability',
and the confusion within the educational and political arenas about the sort of 'account' that is required.   The D.E.S.   11+
Curriculum Enquiry indicates quite clearly that exams
and accountability are linked, however unfortunately.
'If the schools believe their work is appreciated
only as far as it is reflected in exam results, they
will be tempted to subordinate all else ...', as the
Guardian report has it (Guardian Education, 3.8.79).
Some teachers may well feel that schools have already
'subordinated all else' to exam results; though
others seem, in contrast, to feel that exams are the
only satisfactory measure of educational attainment,
and that measurement of educational attainment is
what schools are for.

But within drama teaching there is, and has always
been, an alternative, 'anti-measurement' tradition.
Indeed, there had to be when drama sustained itself
without examinations in the secondary schools, as it
did for some time. The tradition has not always been
particularly sturdy or well-articulated; and it has
not always been expounded or even encouraged by drama
teachers themselves, because they have found themselves, faced by employers, the careers service,
other teachers, heads, parents, and ultimately by
students, with the question 'What use is Drama,?
What is it for?', having to come up with the sort of
answer which will impress that sort of audience; and
that has usually meant something snappy, belonging
rather to the field of public relations than of education: that is, they have often gone for the big
bonanza school play, for performance values, and the
star system in miniature. It has never, sadly, been
thought a reasonable answer, that students enjoy
doing it.

But there has nevertheless been a tradition to which
drama teachers have been able, without too much

special pleading, and with a good deal of integrity,
to appeal. They have been able to point to the work
of the pioneers, Slade and Way, in the more distant
past; and more recently, to a growing corpus of
theoretical work on active learning, co-operative
learning, role-play etc. The Schools Council Projects
such as 'The Arts and the Adolescent' and 'Drama 10-
16' have underwritten most of the positions that
drama teachers have taken up, and generated others
perhaps in advance of what most drama teachers would
claim. Drama has, to some degree, learned to justify
itself without resort to examination criteria as the
media of evaluation.

But this has not been achieved without a price being
paid. Though exam criteria have not been specifically
sustained by these important theoretical bases, nor
have they specifically been excluded; and because
they did set up criteria for evaluation of drama work,
hostages have, so to speak, been offered to the examiners: 'If we can evaluate, then the criteria of
evaluation can be the criteria for examination - out
of one hundred', say the exam freaks. And employers
and careers teachers and teachers of other subjects
and heads and parents and, ultimately, even students,
easily become exam freaks in the present climate.
Drama teachers have thus been caught between the
tradition within their discipline and considerable
pressure within their schools; and have had to decide whether to go with the educational stream, or be
left on the bank with a diminished budget, a diminished option intake, and a diminished role within
their own institution.

In my view, the elements of this conflict are well
illustrated, within the context of the debate on 'A'
level Theatre Studies, in the following exchange between Mike Walton of Hull University Department of
Drama, and Gordon Vallins of South Warwicks College
of F.E. and author of the original AEB Theatre
Studies 'A' level pilot project.

Walton wrote in the Education Guardian

        'The battle for acceptance of drama as
        a subject in schools has almost been

won. What it still appears to lack is
status, and the introduction of 'A'
level studies is seen as a way to improve this. But many teachers believe
that even in 'respectable' academic
subjects, 'A' levels are a poor reflec-
tion of the standards of teaching and
achievement. Why then regiment drama
whose value in schools lies precisely
in its freedom from rigidity and the
competitive nature of working to an
exam structure?

Concentrate on it as a subject that develops emotional and social responses,
which is aesthetic and imaginative, and
even good exercise, and which can enrich the community life of a school.
Encourage an interest in the theatre as
part of the artistic life of a country,
and the drama of any period as a re-
flection of its preoccupations and its
moral attitudes. But at least in
schools let us preserve the subject
from being submerged in the qualifications lottery.'

In an unpublished letter, Vallins replied:

'I agree with Michael Walton that 'the
play's the thing' and that drama can
help develop emotional and social responses which are aesthetic and imaginative and fun and can enrich the life
of any community .... It's true that
to examine a basically free, open, expressive, anarchic and highly personal
subject can be limiting. However, all
examinations have their limitations,
which must be accepted if we approve
the examination system which the universities exploit for extrance qualifications .... In the meantime, I should
like to assure Mr Walton that Drama at
South Warwickshire is far from rigid.
We have an inbred dislike of what has

been called the 'tyranny of subjects'.
We try wherever possible to arrange for
subjects to interact ....'

Vallins goes on to describe areas of interaction:
English, history, art, music; and he ends:

> 'The reason why South Warwickshire pro-
> posed an 'A' level in Theatre Studies
> was simply to give sixteen to nineteen
> year-olds following a course in Drama
> and Liberal Arts the opportunity to gain
> a place in an institution of higher
> education should they wish to apply.
> For some of them, an 'A' level in
> Theatre Studies may be more interesting
> and personally more fulfilling than an
> 'A' level in another subject.'

... Meanwhile Vallins was writing privately to
Walton, making this position more explicit.

> 'Basically, I agree with you ... I will
> be the first in the protest march that
> shouts "Down with exams", but you know
> as well as I do that you would not be
> lecturing at Hull without some kind of
> qualification ...'

Finally, Vallins, in another letter to Walton, out-
lined the problem which I believe was in his mind all
along, but which remains unresolved still.

> 'I shall be very interested to hear the
> outcome of discussions between
> lecturers and drama departments on the
> value of 'A' level Theatre Studies ....
> I don't really want to know about exam-
> inations, but I feel trapped.'

But this correspondence, doesn't only illustrate the
conflict of interests of the drama teacher; it also
illustrates - and concedes - the impotence of the
drama teacher in the face of the zeitgeist - I don't

really want to know about examinations, but I feel
trapped'. I would like to suggest, however, that
this impotence should not be conceded; and that
there are grounds for re-asserting the by no means
feeble anti-exam tradition of drama teaching within
the broad educational context. Moreover, I would
like to challenge the citadel, and ask further the
question: 'Do we need to examine <u>anything</u>?' This
may seem altogether too foolhardy; but I believe
that the examination case is an educational absurdity;
that it is a hermetically sealed system, symbiotically
dependent on the academic system, which it sustains,
and which is sustained by it; and which only a few
subjects, such as drama, relatively untainted by so-
called academic criteria, are in a position to challenge, because they are not dependent on the examination system to sustain them.

It is not easy to do more than outline the sort of
case that can be made, because no one has yet formu-
lated the case fully over the whole educational field,
and yet nothing less than the whole educational field
will give us a position of vantage from which to view
what has happened. However, there are a number of
important elements of the case which have got into
print: the most important of which can be found in
Ronald Dore's 'The Diploma Disease'. Dore's central
proposition is that there has been, and will continue
to be, an inflation of qualification-by-diploma (or
exam), because of the importance that is attached to
the attainment of the diploma/exam, quite independent-
ly of its intrinsic meaning. The greater the importance attached to it, the greater the disjunction between extrinsic and intrinsic meaning, and the more
likely it will be that what is taught will become subordinate to what is examined. There is nothing in
this case that wouldn't be recognized easily by many
teachers; but the force of Dore's argument derives,
not from logical propositions, so much as from his
observation of these propositions working themselves
out in a wide range of differing societies: Japan,
Britain, Tanzania, Cuba and India in particular. In
all of these places, Dore observes the same processes,
and in all of them, he points out that education and
training have tended, in the direct proportion to
which certification has been significant, actually to

de-skill students, making them <u>less</u> well equipped to
respond to their social and economic environments, by
making them pursue goals which are examinable, rather
than intrinsically worthwhile. As a by-product of
his argument, it becomes apparent that the certification industry works primarily to <u>disqualify</u> those
who fail, rather than providing any useful qualifications for those who pass. Inflation follows from
the need to have qualifications, which means that
more and more qualifications are created which mean
less and less; and education as experience loses
value, replaced by education whose only meaning for
students, alienated from what is happening to them,
rests in the hoped for consummation of certification.

Some of these arguments are reflected, often unwit-
tingly, by writers about Drama teaching. Ken Robinson (1977), has put the position with characteristic
irony. "If we have a course which is designed to
'develop the child's whole personality' as some CSE
syllabuses are designated, and if we culminate it
with an examination, I think we should spare some
sympathy for the child who fails. It must be chasten-
ing to become a bad version of yourself, officially".

There are many ways of responding to this irony; but
to me, the passage illustrates the absurd, contra-
dictory drives to which examinations subject us. To
be meaningful, education must deal in serious things;
and comprehensive education must deal in things which
are serious for all; but at the same time, we must
have 'standards', expressed in concepts apparently inseparable from examination - 'Pass' and 'Fail'. Thus
serious and universal concerns drive us in one direction, towards comprehensive education, education of
the whole person in the whole society; while 'standards' drive us, apparently with equal fervour, to
fragmentation into categories of specific and limited
skills, categories of success and failure, categories
of ability. "....We will get nowhere if we restrict
ourselves to....the rat-runner's model of the human
being which everyone knows by personal experience is
comically inadequate, but which many of us have been
trained to accept as convention because it is 'useful'.
I no longer think that it is". (James Hoetker 1975).
In this respect, as in so many others, the Americans

AI - G

seem to have seen the future, to have seen that it
doesn't work, and are preparing to retrace their
steps.

Another drama teacher now working in Canada (a
country which, incidentally, has seen the beginning
of anti-examination legislation in two provinces) has
taken up other elements in Dore's case. Keith Johnstone (1979) for me one of the founding fathers of
educational drama, makes it quite clear that the
creativity of his students is only released if the
normal conditions - and particularly the concept of
failure - can be lifted from the school context: and
that when this condition is provided, co-operation
between student and student, and between teacher and
student, becomes possible: a pre-condition of drama
work. Moreover, Johnstone recognizes that most of
what drama teachers value is at odds with, and indeed
subversive of, the existent educational order. He
is not embarrassed by that recognition: like me, he
believes that it is not drama teaching that is wrong,
but the educational system, which goes about so
heartily to recognize, and then to stigmatise, its
own notions of failure.

I believe another important foundation for the case
against examinations in general can be found in Derek
Rowntree (1977). His argument is, not that we should
not assess students: indeed, he argues in a sense for
more assessment: but that our methods of assessment
have been confused by our determination to 'take for
granted the present nature of assessment, and seek
improvement merely through increasing its efficiency'.
He lists what he takes to be the six general intentions
behind educational assessment: selection, maintaining
standards, motivating students, feedback to students,
feedback to teachers, and 'preparation for life'; and
he demonstrates, among other things, how unreliably
these purposes are fulfilled by the examination system,
and how many side-effects of the system are actually
counter-productive of the intentions of teachers. It
would be impossible to do justice here to the details
of Rowntree's argument: but the book is comprehensible
and easy to read, and I can only believe that teachers
haven't read it either because they are averse to
reading anything about education, or because they

haven't heard of the book (perhaps because vested interests have seen it as too subversive to publicise) or because the teachers themselves see it as an attack on their whole modus operandi, to be ignored if possible.

Rowntree's arguments are of the same order as Witkin's (1974) and Ross's (1974 and 1978). For example: '....The question arises as to whether what can be measured is really what we want to measure - and the answer, at least where the arts are concerned, would seem to be clearly largely in the negative'. (Ross 1978 p.261). As with Rowntree, so with Ross: neither is necessarily against assessment, but both find, in the forms of assessment which are encouraged by examinations, elements quite contrary to the educational intentions which the examinations are (presumably) intended to underpin and sustain. Ross goes on: '....there might be some abilities and attainments that arts teachers really did want to assess - the question is then what they are and how they might be measured........Essentially assessment in the arts:

1. Has to be non-competitive as between one pupil and another.

2. Has to emphasise process skills rather than product finish, knowing rather than knowledge.

3. Must aim to retain rather than lose information about the pupil: is he becoming more himself?

4. Must be arrived at through a joint pupil-teacher dialogue. The moderator's role would have to be totally re-thought.

5. Must balance public with private criteria.

'......In the meantime,......we are well advised to take a very sober and very critical look at the syllabuses available before deciding they are 'good enough' for our pupils. There are radical changes

to be made, and it is the teachers, not the examiners,
who should initiate them .... There comes a time
when the price for 'acceptance' or whatever one may
wish to call it, becomes too high'. Many of Ross's
arguments are taken up in the section of the 1979
N.A.T.D. policy document: 'The Development of Drama
teaching' (N.A.T.D. 1979) on examinations in drama:
in particular the emphasis on 'process' as against
'product', and on groups rather than individuals; but
that document concedes, like Vallins in Appendix 2,
rather than resisting, the hold of the examination
system. On the other hand 'Drama in Scottish Schools'
(HMSO 1977) comes down unequivocally <u>against</u> examinations in drama, whatever the pressure (page 12, para
47); and this document seems to me, not merely more
courageous than the N.A.T.D. document, but also more
far-sighted. I am reluctant to concede that this
far-sightedness may stem from the presence on the
working pary which produced the paper, of non-
teachers: but this would, nevertheless, confirm my
impression that, all too often, it is <u>teachers</u> who
want exams more than anyone, to protect them against
the pervasive meaninglessness of so much of what they
teach.

Meanwhile, Ross has raised important questions and
reservations about the capacity of examinations as
they are generally understood, to assess students'
work in drama. What examination can we think of, in
which dialogue between teacher and students could
conceivably enter into the assessment procedure?
What examination can we think of, which doesn't rig-
orously exclude most of what students can offer in
response, in favour of a very limited notion of what
is suitable? And most of all, what examination do we
know which begins to admit its own accountability by
opening up its assessments to public scrutiny? Have
you ever tried to discover why an individual student
has 'failed'? To know such things would be to pene-
trate the examination mystique: it might show how
little 'objective' basis there often is for the
judgements examiners make 'in camera'; and it might
also help to demonstrate just how reductive an examination has to be, if it is to aspire to objectivity.
'But', the examiners will say, 'the exams are much
too important, and far too much depends on them, for

them to be open to the prying eyes of every teacher,
parent and student in the land'. Conversely, of
course, if they <u>were</u> open to such scrutiny, and the
ridicule which might follow, they might cease to be
quite so important. Their importance is sustained by
their secrecy, and their secrecy, by their importance.
Only some sort of 'leap in the dark', and Ross
suggests that it might be made by teachers, can break
this closed system. But I don't think it need be an
entirely existentialist leap, at any rate for drama
teachers, who can be confident that the subject they
teach does have intrinsic satisfactions for students:
who know that the values for which drama stands are
traduced by the examination process, and who have to
hand, therefore, both the power and the understanding
to force the breach of what often seems the impreg-
nable fortress of public examinations, and to establish a bridgehead across which real, intrinsically
valuable education can be established in the years a-
head.

Or is this too heroic a picture? I am certainly unable to play the 'God for Harry' role myself: more a
Scrope of Masham. In the college in which I taught
drama for eight years, I ended up teaching almost
every examination syllabus in sight, because within
that institution the pressure to teach such courses
seemed irresistable. My failure to resist the tide
was instrumental in persuading me to leave that
college; but it is a tide which pervades practically
the whole of education.

For its early years, the Theatre Studies 'A' level
looked as though it would in some ways escape at
least the worst aspects of examination, because it
was a syllabus which appeared to be devised by
teachers who were interested in students' learning.
But the new, Schools Council approved syllabus now
devised by A.E.B. has the mark of the professional
examiner upon it: prescriptive and unadventurous in
its limited choice of texts, academic in its introduction of specific historical periods to be 'taught',
excluding creative writing from the list of acceptable practical submissions, and, in its introduction
of the unseen passage for commentary and analysis,
moving towards a stimulus/response model of critical

activity which makes life easy for examiners, but
difficult for candidates.

I must confess to having felt betrayed by the new
syllabus; but I think I was wrong to expect anything
other than a shift of emphasis of the sort I have
described. What should one do now? On what ground
should we stand?

For myself, seeing drama drawn into the examination
miasma, I have retreated, like Hereward the Wake, into an island in the Fens, to a post whose responsibility is entirely for non-examined courses. For me
to give up a Head of Drama post is no great sacrifice,
because I think almost any teaching job can be a
drama teaching one - and anyway, I was never that
good at the drama bits. Each drama teacher, each
teacher of a creative subject, each creative teacher,
each teacher who hopes that within his or her work in
the classroom there is some creative potential for
the students who survive there, has to negotiate his
or her own terms of existence; but I believe that
the common ground of the non-examined curriculum must
be held, and that that ground is most easily and
effectively held by those subjects and activities of
which the demands, and the satisfactions, are intrinsic to the activities themselves; and I believe that
it is, therefore, a ground which creative arts teachers can hold, and must share with whoever offers to
join them.

REFERENCES

Dore, Ronald (1976). The Diploma Disease. Allen and
    Unwin.

Hoetker, James (1975). Researching Drama: an American
    View, in Teaching and Understanding Drama.
    Stephenson and Vincent (Eds.), N.F.E.R.

Johnstone, Keith (1979). Impro. Faber and Faber.

Robinson, Ken.,(1977). Drama in the Secondary School,
    Cockpit Arts Workshop.

Ross, Malcolm (1975). The Arts and the Adolescent,
     Evans-Methuen.

Ross, Malcolm (1978). The Creative Arts. Heinemann.

Rowntree, Derek (1977). Assessing Students. How
     Shall we know them? Harper and Rowe.

Witkin, Robert W.,(1974). The Intelligence of
     Feeling. Heinemann.

Education and the Arts
Are Schools the Enemy?

HARRY RÉE

Preamble

By serving as Chairman of the Schools Council Music
Project's Consultative Committee I learned how badly
schools encourage the development of imagination,
sensitivity and inventiveness. Because schools are
not concerned to develop feelings. Feelings cannot
be competitively examined. Opinions about 'accepted'
products of the Arts are taught; the process of
teaching (?) Arts subjects generally ensures rejection of and by the majority. Schools are ridden with
exam 'requirements' and with unbendable timetables
which offer snippets of time unsuitable for the pursuit of the Arts. Recognize that it is the frills
which make a lasting impression while the regular
timetabled subjects leave little deposit. Recognize
the desirability of mixing up adults with the young,
parents with their children, for the practice of the
Arts, which points the way forward to community
schools and permanent education.

****

As far as the Arts are concerned, I might be called a
cultured philistine - don't disbelieve me. I almost
never feel ecstasy when confronted by a picture, a
sculpture or a piece of music. I cannot act or

compose or design or paint. When I read the Intelligence of Feeling in MS I found the language so obscure
- (much too obscure for the teacher on the Clapham
omnibus) - that I recommended that Mr Witkin should
look for an outside publisher rather than it being
the responsibility of the Schools Council to publish
it.

I haven't yet finished my apology - I said I am a cultured philistine - there are thousands of us, alas,
formed and modelled by our education to <u>speak</u> re-
spectfully of the arts, to be bespattered with a
smattering of Art History, to make an attempt to take
innovation on board, and to reproduce ourselves in
the next generation. We do this by introducing our
children to established art through inculcating in
them an apparent respect for museums, art galleries
and churches, and an open, even welcoming, mind when
meeting living artists, or when seeing or hearing
their work for the first time.

I must admit to one salutary and important influence
when I was still not totally hardened off, still in
the plastic state - I came to know and be friends
with Henry Morris, Chief Education Officer for Cam-
bridgeshire from 1922 to 1954. He was often ecstatic
about the arts - he would meditate happily in a Flor-
entine Church which was totally empty save for a few
little urchins playing up by the chancel, would listen
wrapped in delight to Mozart, and once told the
chairman of a Northern Education Committee, when vis-
iting one of his new schools, where a reproduction of
the Sun Flowers had pride of place in the entrance
hall: "I'd rather hang a dead cat on the wall than a
reproduction." But Henry wasn't an art teacher - he
once told the head of a village college to take the
childrens' pictures off the walls of the entrance
hall because it made the place look like a school!
Not an art teacher, not therefore constrained by a
school, but for me, and many others, he was a teacher,
and a remarkable builder of schools and colleges
where creation and re-creation would, he hoped, be
actively encouraged, and where, what he called, the
production and consumption of the Arts, would be a
principal feature. On the establishment of such new
institutions he wrote: (Harry Rée, 1973)

"Our species, in solving the problem of
poverty and overwork is in fact moving
forward to a more perilous stage in its
history .... Universal comfort with
wealth and repletion .... is the next
great problem for homo sapiens. Words
cannot do justice to the urgency and
wisdom of thinking out new institutions
to enable communities to face this new
situation.

We are in the presence of a vast cultural breakdown, and nowhere is this more
evident than in the collapse of our
visual environment .... We live without
complaint in a wasteland of un-art."

And he warned of: "the menace of aimless leisure a-
midst economic security, and of the decadence and
disillusion and weariness that will arise with widespread intellectual and emotional unemployment."

But besides my close association with a man of vision
like Henry Morris, you may well be justified in
thinking that I have some qualification for talking
here through my having been chairman of the Consultative Committee of John Paynter's Secondary School
Music Project.
Well,   I'll   admit   that   over   the   past   six
years in that Chair I've learned a lot about the way
music is and might be taught, but once more I've not
got any musical qualifications for doing that job -
in fact this was the reason John asked me to take it
on. When I protested to him, he explained that if
his project team could convince ME that their ideas
would work they'd be half way to success - half way
was right, because I've come to realise that the project still has a long way to go. But I did in fact
realise that what John Paynter wanted me for was the
fact that, although I am ignorant of music, I do know
about schools and that I have a prejudice, tendency
perhaps would be a more polite word, to regard education as inclusive rather than exclusive, and this in-
clusiveness is one of the most important aspects of
the Paynter Project, recognising - in that happy
phrase used by Jann Howarth - "the resident artist

in all of us."

So I'll stop apologizing now for my inadequacies, and
admit that I come to this task of talking to you on
this subject almost with relish, because I have got a
message. I want to put forward the point of view
I've already partly hinted at, using myself as an example, that schools are not places well suited to
Education in the Arts. Although some succeed with
some pupils, most make a hash of it, and probably the
ones who are succeeding could do better; in fact I'll
suggest one possible way of overcoming the disadvantages of trying to teach or promote the Arts in a
school before I've finished. In the meantime, may I
explain a little more clearly why I feel that schools
don't do very well as promoters of the Arts and sometimes do actual harm.

Promotion of the Arts, (would you agree?) aims to develop imagination, sensitivity, inventiveness and delight, and works largely and most effectively through
the feelings. But schools, for several understand-
able reasons, are not geared to work through the
feelings - the very opposite. They are designed to
impart information, to reward exactitude, to incul-
cate skills and sometimes to develop curiosity. They
are then expected to test the outcomes of their
teaching and give numerical evidence for the success
or failure of themselves or their pupils. But the
development of feelings cannot be tested by formal
examinations, and imagination is the enemy of exactitude. I recall the experience of a little grand-
child of mine who came back from her primary school
one afternoon, crying, and when my daughter asked
what was wrong she said she'd been naughty. Sympathetic, my daughter asked what had happened: "Miss
told us to draw an animal with horns. I drew a rab-
bit with horns, and she was cross and sent me out of
the room." I'm not saying that is typical, but what
is certain is that schools, because of circumstances
almost beyond their control, have downgraded imagination and, therefore, the arts.

These circumstances have led schools traditionally to
prize the thinker and look down on the doer, prize
the imitator and re-producer, and look down on the

innovator and originator. Because of this tendency
it has been argued recently that we have failed, not
merely to encourage the arts in schools, we have
failed to encourage the skills of the imaginative de-
signer and the development of practical engineering.
But we must leave that problem to Sir Monty Finniston,
for there are other points worth mentioning. Where
schools have made an effort to introduce arts subjects
- (subject differentiation is another anti-educational
idea) into the curriculum they have done so with the
aim of producing - nurturing - 'cultivated individuals'. I know about this, because it was done to me,
and turned me into what I've termed a cultivated
philistine. They set out to produce people who will
know the difference between Beethoven and Bartok, between Vermeer and Van Gogh, between Swan Lake and
the Firebird - to this end they set about inculcating
facts about the arts, by the well tried process they
are so good at, of laying thin films of information
across the minds of pupils and training them to peel
them off at the appropriate moment, in the exam room,
to lay them out, dead and cold, for the benefit of
the examiners of the Oxbridge or A level General
Paper. In this way they develop in some pupils the
knowledge of what can be accepted as art, and even go
so far as to indicate a league table of artists,
where of course, Shakespeare, Beethoven and Leonardo
are captains of their respective first elevens. But
although this might be thought to be as harmless an
exercise as a course in Pulchritude, it does in fact
constitute a recipe for dishonesty, and is little more
than a course in anaesthetic appreciation. It is
particularly suited to the production of ladies and
gentlemen who, after all, must learn to stifle their
innermost feelings in public, and sometimes, also,
(poor dears!) in private. Conversely it is highly
unsuitable for kids who haven't the slightest interest in becoming ladies and gentlemen, and who find
the taking of endless notes on the great musicians,
or listening to records they find 'dead boring', a
perfect excuse for rejecting what's being offered.

While on the subject of rejection, another stifling
result of schooling in the arts is the process, as
with languages (or indeed almost with any traditional
subject) of pupil rejection, that is, rejection of

the pupils by the school. A large proportion of
those who begin a subject in schools are forewarned
that they are bound to fail - bound to be pushed off
the course before they have completed it. A corol-
lory of this is that a small minority only is able to
retain their places. This may be admissable in a
world where the job of schools is seen as a means of
sorting out the winners, admissable perhaps in a subject like languages. (In fact, considering the way
languages are usually taught in schools this is almost inevitable.) But in the Arts, this rejection
process, so well established especially in music, is
crassly stupid. In fact, if you can bear a short
parenthesis, I'ld like to make a little comparative
study of the teaching of French and Music, which may
be relevant and instructive for those concerned with
promoting the Arts in schools.

As I became familiar with the Music Project I began
to notice the similarity between teaching music in
schools and teaching French in schools. For some
years I have been aware that French teachers were at
a disadvantage as compared with the teachers of most
other subjects, because, however hard they tried,
they knew that there was a much better place than the
classroom to learn French, and that was in France -
in the bosom of a French family talking French all
the time.

I also noticed that French teachers were remarkably
unsuccessful at getting more than a minority of
pupils even through to O level standard, let alone
get them to a stage where they could understand or
talk French or write it. This had caused teachers to
expect the majority of those whom they started off
with to drop out after a couple of years, to the
great relief of the same teachers and their victims.

One of the additional disadvantages of teaching a
language was that to do it effectively pupils had to
make a noise - they had to talk and hear you talk -
but this made discipline difficult - so in order to
'keep order' the teacher was tempted to get the
children <u>writing</u> far more than was good for their
learning of French. In fact the only ones one did
have any success with were those who actually wanted

to learn, and whose parents were often behind them.
We were in fact selecting the volunteers.

I hope you can see now the interesting similarity between the task of the French teacher and the task of
the Music teacher. They both know that there are
better places for 'learning' their subject. They know
they are teaching eventually, a minority subject.
They both make disturbing noises (disturbing for colleagues) and indeed the noises they want the pupils
to make with their voices are, in each case, for many
children, an inhibiting emotional experience which is
naturally resisted.

But there is one great difference, which is too often
disregarded by the teachers of music, and which can,
and should, be used to their advantage. No child to
whom you are teaching French actually HAS French before you start - if you do have a French speaker as a
pupil in your class you quickly get rid of them! But
... you get the point. All the pupils in your music
class have got music - only a tiny minority don't involve themselves willingly and almost continuously in
music OUT OF SCHOOL. I know it's not establishment
music, it's pop or reggae, or rock or perhaps jazz -
but it IS music, and this is where John Paynter takes
off. He recognises the "resident musician" in each
child and proceeds to set it to work. And because
among the music establishment this kind of original/
primitive music is distasteful/disdained/rejected,
they tend to reject Paynter, and totally misjudge
what he is trying to do. I must stop any of you who
are unfamiliar with the project from thinking that
Paynter starts and stops with pop music - what he
does do is to start with the kids' home-made music -
music they make themselves - sounds they make themselves which MAY be related to their own kind of music
- but which in the first instance may be patterns of
sounds made with hands or voices and odd instruments
that are available. But the music is THEIR own, and
the pop, reggae etc. can well come along into the
classroom at any time, and it wont be rejected. Nor,
of course, will the traditional musician, who is welcome as an additional resource, welcome in a way that
the French speaker in the beginners French class wont
be. But what a fight it has been to get this approach

accepted by the music establishment. The enemy are
not just gathered at the gates, they're inside the
citadel - and they are most powerful figures - inspectors, advisers, teacher trainers, examiners, all
of whom pride themselves on producing within and outside schools selected examples of musical excellence,
and to hell with the hoi-polloi; they regard John Paynter as being against all that they stand for. Of course
they're wrong, because John's approach is inclusive,
and he welcomes the gifted cellist or flautist, (who
hasn't relied on the school so much as private lessons to bring them up to high standards) who are now
well on their way to Pimlico, or the musical Bluecoats
School in Manchester or the Yehudi School in Chobham.
With Paynter they are brought into the classroom as
collaborators, who not only teach but learn from the
primitive learners.

Other enemies inside the schools are the Heads, who
tend to expect, like any normal school-person, each
subject department to produce winners and to exhibit
them, to the greater glory of the school. The
academics can only display their O and A level results
while some 'lucky' Heads have a few Oxbridge Scholar-
ships to pin up, but even these are less showy than
the exhibition in the entrance hall, or the concert
on Speech Day, or in some rare cases, the crowning
glory, the appearance at the Schools Prom.

So once more, those responsible for the Arts in
schools, and especially the musicians, or the drama
teacher, are pressed into selection and rejection,
simply because they are working in schools.

There is one further impediment imposed by schools to
the proper free development of the arts, and this is
the damned timetable, where the arts teacher, and
each pupil, are forced to break into the production
or the rehearsal, into the act of creation in painting or printing or potting, at the sound of a bell or
a tannoy, in order to get to school dinner, or to
maths or P.E.

I wont go on with this catalogue of impedements and
disadvantages. I must only have been reminding most
of you of a fact that is already familiar, reminding

you of how difficult it is to do your job as you
would like to do it. I'm assuming of course that you
agree that the last thing a promoter of the arts
needs to be is a rejector - needs to look on a proportion of the kinds they 'teach' as 'unteachable'.
I am myself convinced of the existence of the resistant artist in all and that each human being can be
brought, as they grow up through the latency period,
and through puberty to an adult state where imagination, sensitivity, inventiveness and delight can be
developed through feeling and emotion. And should be.
Convinced that all human beings can produce and con-
sume what the Arts can offer at one level or another,
and that it is the job of teachers to bring them to
this happy land.

But how can we do it in schools? With difficulty,
that's certain. But I'ld like to suggest two ways we
might make it easier. And I'm not suggesting a total
deschooling of the arts, but we must surely work to
transform, even if only slightly and by stages, our
existing schools.

If we look back on our schooldays, what were the moments when something really important and memorable
happened? And where were you when it happened? In
the classroom? Doubtful. More likely in a play, a
concert or on a theatre visit. On an excursion, at
camp along with friends and a teacher you were getting
to know. But these events are regarded as frills, as
peripheral little stopping places on our long educational trip. But the experience of many people
points to the fact that such moments are central to
learning and, therefore, what we should begin to do
is to turn the school inside out - put the peripheral
experience into the middle, and put the classroom experience on the fringe.

Here's a possible way to start doing this. It's a
trick, if you like, and it's an idea you need to
sell; you need to get the idea into the Head's head
that what is needed once in a while, once a term, or
at the start perhaps only once a year, is a whole
week, during term time, when the timetable is in fact
broken; when each member of staff offers to organise
an activity to any volunteers, an activity which will

capitalise each teacher's enthusiasm - it may result
in a trip by a group to St Malo or Morocco, a field
trip to Malham Tarn or the Western Isles, a course in
photography or the production of a local newspaper.
Arts teachers could have the whole week consuming and
producing their arts in a planned,sequential and perhaps co-operative way, with no breaks or unwanted
interruptions.

The second suggestion is related to my own lifelong
enthusiasm for lifelong education - for community
education which was sparked off by Henry Morris when
I was working with him in Cambridge during a long vac
term. Promotion of the Arts by teachers can be
effective with people of all ages, and often it is
good to have adults involved with children, in the
same place, on the same project. This is difficult
in a normal school, but in a community college, or
better still perhaps, in a community arts centre,
whether connected or not with a college, promotion of
the arts for all ages can flourish.

What I've been saying is that we need to listen again
to Illich - he got a bad press when he first crossed
the Atlantic because people felt that what he was re-
commending was an all out destruction of schools as
they were, and this was clearly impossible even if
some people thought it a desirable goal. But we can
compromise, we can modify the disadvantages of school,
and I can't help feeling that arts teachers, instead
of sitting down under the difficulties of promoting
the arts in schools, ought to spend a bit of time
taking down   (or putting time bombs under) the ob-
stacles and barricades against the arts which schools
traditionally put up. And then persuading people,
starting perhaps with their colleagues, that our aim
should be to bring schools back to what they once
were - places where people constructively and willingly spend their leisure. For let me end on an academic
note   -   the Greek word skoles, from which we get
our word school, means leisure, and in a civilised
society leisure involves working for love.

AI - H

The Reconstruction of English as Art

PETER ABBS

It is a difficult business cutting through and going
beyond what is safely established. Merely to locate
what has been excluded in current thinking is taxing,
but to take what has been excluded and to bring it
into controversial relationship with what is current
in order to find a synthesis greater than both, that
seems all but impossible to achieve. And yet with
regards to English teaching that is now the task con-
fronting us.

In this essay my main intention will be to argue for
a concept of English as a literary - expressive discipline, a discipline whose deepest affinities lie
not with the Humanities (as has been commonly conceived) but with the Arts or what I prefer to call,
at least in the context of the curriculum, the Expressive Disciplines. One of the most important
claims I will make is that English should now form
strong philosophical, practical and political
alliances with the undervalued disciplines of Art,
Drama, Dance, Music and Film. More specifically, I
would like to see English teachers turn in a new
manner (though, as we shall see, not uninformed by
the best in the rich, uneven heritage of English
teaching) to the expressive dimension in order to
sustain and develop the neglected emotional and imaginative energies of their pupils; and to do this,
not in superior isolation (as was often the habit of
the Cambridge School of English) but in vivid, open
and generous collaboration with those other departments in the school, college or university likewise
committed to the expressive and inner life of the
student.

For reasons that will become clearer as we proceed,
sustained collaborative work and sustained collaborative exchange between the Expressive Disciplines
seldom takes place at the secondary level of education with the result that the arts in our schools
have lacked philosophical coherence, organisational
unity and practical bite. I think it is not a matter
of contention but of simple description to say that
no child by design (or, perhaps, even by chance) receives in the state system anything resembling a true
aesthetic education. Although one could document
many fine exceptions, the Expressive Disciplines in
our schools are in a state of confusion, neglect,
poverty, demoralization and absurd fragmentation.
The Expressive Disciplines lie on the very periphery
of the curriculum; in most schools they are not even
regarded with the traditional suspicion, they are not
even noticed. According to formal DES figures,
about 10% of the total curriculum at secondary level
is given to the arts, but, given the way in which
many of the arts are actually taught, it would be
reasonable to assume that only half of this time is
devoted to genuinely expressive tasks, i.e. about 5%
of the total time given to the curriculum is directly
engaged with aesthetic experience. Furthermore, in
many secondary schools, where an optional system operates after the third year, the arts can and frequently do disappear completely from the education of
the adolescent.

I believe that such a dramatic restriction of the
aesthetic-expressive dimension calls for a reappraisal
of the meaning of English.

At memorable points in the past, as I shall attempt
to show, the nature of English has been seen as literary and expressive. From almost the beginning of
the century Caldwell Cook linked English with Drama
and, more generally, with enactment, embodiment and
expressive presentation. Under the impetus of what I
will name the Progressive Movement in English teaching, innumerable teachers have intuitively felt
(rather than conceptually realized) that English belongs most naturally with the epistemic community of
the Arts. In Primary schools, particularly, the con-
nections between literature, song, imagery, painting

sculpture, drama, mime, were spontaneously forged in
the practice of good teaching. In this essay I will
critically and sympathetically analyse earlier traditions in the teaching of English in order to sal-
vage some of the elements necessary for its reconstitution. But this will not be sufficient. In
order to make our case convincing it will be necessary to examine the dominant theories of the last fifteen years. This will be contentious.   It is not,
I think, a caricature to suggest that frequently in
the last twenty years English has been envisaged
either as Linguistics or Social Studies. In the
first case, it has suffered from an intolerable
narrowing: in the second, from an intolerable dif-
fusion and a dangerous distortion. In both versions
English has severed its potentially rich connection
with the Arts. It is symptomatic of the present
state that although English may have reached across
the curriculum, it never entered, as an energizing
force, the teaching of the Expressive Disciplines,
nor has it given any serious attention to the nature
of the aesthetic. Even in the study of literature,
there has been a tendency, among leading theorists,
to reduce imaginative art to the level of mere sociological manifestation and social class phenomena.
These strictures are severe. And are intended to be.
Yet it would be grossly wrong-headed not to recognize
in the current orthodoxies some major compelling insights into educational practice, into that elusive
process we call 'learning'. But this is to antici-
pate my argument ....

I am, then, concerned with a revaluation and a reform-
ulation of English. Only by an examination of previous formulations, only by a relentless thinking
down to informing principles, can we secure the conditions necessary for the growth of educational disciplines. The practical possibilities not only unfold in the classroom (although what happens there is
crucial) they also unfold out of deep insight into
living principle, into the intrinsic nature of what
it is we seek to do. Paradoxically, if we are to
take the chains off the present state of English, we
must go back and down, back to half-forgotten formulations, down to underlying principles. This must be
the first exercise in any reconstruction.

2.

Although, as D.H. Lawrence claimed, logic is far too coarse to make the subtle distinctions life demands, yet in an area as contentious and problematic as English teaching, a few opening definitions are called for. Often the uncertainty of aims which attends English teaching derives from little more than the ambiguity of its own title. For the word English has a number of possible references. Even in its educational context it can possess at least three distinct meanings:

1. English as a second language

2. English as the mother-tongue and medium of nearly all teaching and learning

3. English as a discipline in its own right, as a distinct symbolic form, e.g. English as studied at a University.

In this essay I will not be concerned with English as a foreign language. I will consider the notion as English as a medium and, in particular, the current demand for 'Language across the curriculum' which I will fully endorse. But, essentially, I am pre-occupied with English as a discipline. One of the problems with current theories about English is that it tends not to differentiate between discipline and medium, or rather, it tends to dissolve the discipline into the medium. Thus the English teacher becomes responsible for all kinds of language and all kinds of learning. He becomes a general adviser rather than an initiator into a specific kind of knowing through a specific kind of procedure and through a specific kind of language. The English teacher thus becomes like a man carrying a bag of tools but with only other people's jobs to do. Such a view I will argue, while having undoubted strengths, is totally inadequate. It leaves out the meaning of the discipline; it discards or demotes the unique contribution English has to make as a symbolic form.

The important distinction I want to establish is that
between discipline (or symbolic form) and medium (the
language necessary for nearly all kinds of learning).
With this at the back of our minds, we can now turn
to examine the three main traditions in English
teaching: the Progressive Movement, the Cambridge
School of English and the current Socio-Linguistic
School. I am going to argue that while no one movement offers a comprehensive account of English, each
has offered certain vivifying principles, which
brought together provide us with most of the elements
necessary for a radical yet inwardly consistent transformation of the subject. I will work historically,
taking each   movement in its chronological order,
but, as I have explained, my interests are heuristic
and not documentary. I am not concerned with the
actual description of the whole rock only the valuable mineral which can be extracted and used in a
new context. After all, in education our main concern is the transformation of inherited culture according to our deep existential needs. So, first, we
take the Progressives ....

                        3.

The Progressive Movement in English teaching goes
back almost to the beginning of this century. In
its early stages (1910 -1925) some of its key expo-
nents were: Percy Nunn, Greening Lamborn, Edmund
Holmes, W.S. Tomkinson and Caldwell Cook. As early
as 1911 Edmund Holmes had written in What Is and What
Might Be:

> 'For a third of a century, from 1862-
> 95, self-expression on the part of the
> child may be said to have been for-
> mally prohibited by all who were re-
> sponsible for the elementary education
> of the children of England, and also
> to have been prohibited de facto by all
> the unformulated conditions under which
> the elementary school was conducted.'

Self-expression prohibited. That was the cry and

challenge of the Progressive Movement in English.
Against the mechanical forms of teaching, the Progressives asserted the need for a freer and more
spontaneous approach allowing the child to generate
much of the curriculum according to his creative
needs. Characteristically, in his book Holmes con-
demns without qualification the external examination
system complaining 'of its tendency to arrest growth,
to deaden life, to paralyse the higher faculties, to
externalize what is inward, to materialize what is
spiritual' and 'to involve education in an atmosphere of unreality and self-deception'. The critique bears within it its own positive conception of
education: as the unfolding and elaboration of self
through activity, intellectual enquiry and creative
play.

The movement largely derived its thinking from Montessori, Froebel, Herbart, Pestalozzi and ultimately
from Rousseau. Caldwell Cook's 'Begin with the Child'
powerfully echoes Emile, Rousseau's influential
charter for children. The concepts 'growth', 'self-
expression', 'individuality', 'play', litter the
works of these early pioneers. As the movement developed so it absorbed into itself ideas from psycho-
analysis, particularly from Freud and Jung. It culminated in two highly influential works, Herbert
Read's Education through Art (1943) and Marjorie
Hourd's Education of the Poetic Spirit (1949).

The strength of the Progressive Movement was to emphasise the power of creativity in education, to recognize the place of feeling and of imagination, to
perceive the value of psychic wholeness. In 1921
W.S. Tomkinson in The Teaching of English: A New
Approach referred to reading as 'a creative art' and
to the child as a maker who 'strives after the expression of himself and does it in the same way as
the poet - by creative work'. Both of these claims
remain quite central. It is important to notice
also that in this first major move to give English a
creative shape, there is an implicit recognition
that English belongs with the arts. For Caldwell
Cook writing plays, acting, modelling, drawing,
painting are part of the same inextricable pattern

or paradigm. In <u>The Education of the Poetic Spirit</u>
the teaching of Drama and the teaching of English are
both explored and are seen to be part of the same
quest for the symbolic ordering of elusive experience
(and thus the refining of that experience). Although
there is little conceptual understanding of the
nature of the relationship between the arts, there is
an intuitive recognition of their common identity so
that the teaching of English, Drama and even Art not
only run often side by side but interpenetrate, becoming different facets of the same motion. From
this practice we have a great deal to relearn. We
have allowed specialization and the consequent fragmentation of the curriculum into a thousand jost-
ling bits to destroy the collaborative spirit which
should characterise the teaching of similar forms of
symbolic activity. Thirty minutes of Drama here;
one hour of Art there; some Music somewhere else;
lessons of eclectic English scattered throughout the
week; we have ended up not with a coherent curriculum but a liquorice allsort confusion. The Progressives were on the right track in emphasising unity
and organic form and in intuitively grouping the
Arts as members of the same epistemic community.

At the same time, it is impossible not to be aware
of the crippling weaknesses of the Progressive
English teachers. I think it is just to say that
they possessed an effusive concept of the child, at
once intolerably vague and hugely indulgent. In
their minds the poet and the child become synony-
mous, yet the poet both expresses and extends his
own culture in a way no child can possibly do. There
was no critical theory of culture and, while there
was a great appreciation of spontaneity, there was
no correcting appreciation of critical methods, of
ordered and sustained analysis.

There was an inflated view of human nature which
gave birth to an almost unhealthy idealism. 'In
Utopia', wrote Edmund Holmes, 'the training which
the child receives may be said to be based on the
doctrine of original goodness'. He saw an 'infinite
capacity for good' but failed to detect the shadow
which all light inevitably casts. He failed to grasp
the perplexities, the irrationalities, the deep

ambivalences of the human soul. This is not the
place to explore, in responsible detail, the defects
of the progressive ideology - many of them deriving
from that Philistine of Genius, Rousseau - but those
defects weakened considerably the movement I have
been describing. At worst it culminated in a sentimental indulgence of the child's every whim, a building of the curriculum on the sands of chance impulse
and immediate gratification. Often it served best
as therapy rather than education. And yet in courageously insisting on the primacy of feeling, the Progressives defended the deep springs from which authentic art, whether in English or Music, Drama or Art,
derives. The life of impulse was central to the Progressives and it is the key to the Expressive Disciplines. Without some impulse desiring expression
in order to know itself, there can be no authentic
art-making. The movement of art-making runs from
emotion to medium to symbolic form to the integration
of the original emotion and its contemplation. In
celebrating feeling, and in placing feeling at the
heart of education, the Progressives were responsible
for restoring human energies which had been long
suppressed and maligned, particularly by educational
theorists. In beginning to integrate the formidable
and unsettling insights of Freud and Jung into the
theory and practice of teaching (as in the case of
Marjorie Hourde, Marion Milner, Seonaid Robertson,
Herbert Read) they also helped to institute a new
kind of understanding about knowing and relating
which we have still to develop and make clear. As
Marjorie Hourd was the first to recognize, the insights coming from psycho-analysis had a major bearing on the way in which English could be reconstitu-
ted, the way in which children's writing could be
interpreted, the way in which Drama and Literature
worked, the way in which the English teacher could
relate to the inherent ambivalences in adolescent
emotion in order to make possible the education of
the poetic spirit. Perhaps the great sanity of the
Progressive Movement is concentrated in Herbert
Read's conviction:

> 'The secrets of our collective ills is
> to be traced to the suppression of spon-
> taneous creative ability in the individual'

And yet ...   And yet spontaneity also requires,
paradoxically, discipline and a bed of culture. Without form, without tradition, without a fund of exem-
plary symbols, the creative impulse becomes lean,
autistic, exiled. To understand the nature of these
complementary qualities we must turn to the next
major reconstitution of English, made within a
different tradition and in the context of the study
of English at University, the Cambridge School.

4.

If the Progressive Movement had its line of descent
running backwards from Montessori to Froebel to Herbert to Pestallozi to Rousseau, that is, into one
European philosophical and pedagogic tradition, the
Cambridge School, centred on the work of F.R. Leavis,
remained stolidly English, running back into the work
of George Sampson, Matthew Arnold, and, to a lesser
extent, Coleridge. The greatness of the Cambridge
School was to keep alive and make muscular the 19th
century Arnoldian literary-critical tradition. Out
of the practice of I.A. Richards, the Cambridge critics developed a critical method, a procedure for
reading with sensitive accuracy, feeling and due discrimination, works of literature. They provided,
along with T.S. Eliot and Ezra Pound, a more coherent
sense of the continuous organic tradition of English
literature. In new and worsening cultural circumstances the Cambridge School gave powerful currency
to the notion that the teacher, critic and artist
had no choice but to oppose the destructive and seemingly inexorable drift of industrial civilisation.
As George Sampson (1921) had trenchantly written in
English for the English:

> I am prepared to maintain, and indeed,
> do maintain without reservation or per-
> hapses, that it is the purpose of edu-
> cation, not to prepare children for their
> occupations, but to prepare children
> against their occupations.

This defiant antagonism to the dehumaning effects of

the industrial revolution permeates the Cambridge
School. It issued in an insistence on the need to
generate in the young the habit of cultural discrimination and an awareness of the English literary
tradition which, in its profound engagement with
fundamental human dilemmas and possibilities, embodied true alternatives to the crass hedonism and sharp
technicism of our own times.

As the Cambridge School owes much of its inspiration
and many of its characteristic concerns to F.R.
Leavis, it is necessary to attempt here a brief
evaluation of Leavis' contribution to English. I
will consider first what I regard to be the positive
aspects,   then move to some of the
more negative features. I will argue that while the
Cambridge School does not provide us with a sufficiently comprehensive concept of English, it does
provide us with those elements of criticism and cultural heritage which the Progressives had either ignored or rejected, elements quite crucial to any
reconstitution of the subject.

There can, I think, be little doubt that F.R. Leavis
was a great English critic, one of the few and one of
the best in our century. His greatness, though,
rests not so much on the versatility and fertility
of his mind, as on its passionate stubborness over
a few principles. Here is a critic who knew a few
things, we might say, but knew them with the whole
energy of his being. This insistence on certain premises, sustained throughout a life-time, conferred a
narrowness to his writing but within that narrowness
there developed a fierce consistency, challenging,
disturbing, uncompromising.

Leavis in the first place and most obviously, believed in the potential energy of significant literature as exerting a formative pressure on existence.
Because of this he argued that there could be no
division between aesthetics and life, between beauty
and meaning. Art comes out of life and returns us
(often at a heightened level) to it. The critic
holding such a position is often dubbed a 'moral-
ist' or called 'puritanical'. Such a response is
surely evasive, indicating an unwillingness to face

the demanding nature of literature, which inevitably, intends meaning. For if we consider the nature
of language itself, we discover two interdependent
aspects, a power to denote and a power to connote,
that is, a power both to refer and to express a
feeling about that which is referred to. The writer
using language, in a personal and charged manner,
will, by the very nature of his medium, fuse both
aspects. In insisting on the moral nature of literature, Leavis reminded an age, sinking into the desolate march of egalitarianism, of the power of the
creative word to promote consciousness and conscience.
He has also carried the tradition of moral criticism,
which runs from Johnson to Arnold, into our own confused century. This in itself was an achievement
difficult to overestimate.

In fact, tradition is a vital concern in Leavis'
writing. His criticism points us not to a number of
isolated geniuses, but to an organic English tradition out of which humus the great literary works have
grown. Leavis constantly reminds us that a writer
labours within a context and that there is a crucial
interplay between the two. On the one side, the
writer keeps the language alert and sensitive, on
the other side, the state of the language, which the
writer inherits, opens or restricts his range and
his impact. Commenting on D.H. Lawrence, Leavis
(1975) writes:

>   Without the English language waiting
>   quick and ready for him, Lawrence could-
>   n't have communicated his thought: that
>   is obvious enough. But it is also the
>   case that he couldn't have thought it.
>   English as he found it was a product of
>   an immemorial 'sui generis' collabora-
>   tion on the part of its speakers and
>   writers. It is alive with promptings
>   and potentialities, and the great cre-
>   ative writer shows his genius in the
>   way he responds. Any writer of the
>   language must depend on what his read-
>   ers know already (though they may not
>   know that they know) - must evoke it
>   with the required degree of sharpness

or latency.

The extent to which the writer can advance consciousness, the sensitive, articulate life of the
whole man and woman, depends, to a large extent, on
the general state of the culture which surrounds him.
An exhausted language can only support an exhausted
art. A sensitivity to the state of the language -
to its possible resonances, its underflow of meaning,
its current of associations, its historical burden -
becomes, by implication, not only the hallmark of
the good writer, but also of the good reader critic
and teacher, all of whom work the language in the
name of vision, insight, individual depth, and ade-
quacy of understanding.

For Leavis there is another important and related
condition necessary for the development of the writer. If his work is to develop he requires an
audience, a dedicated minority, quick to appreciate
his intentions and ready to evaluate them as they
are embodied in his actual works. If the writer has
such an audience he has, again, secured one of the
critical conditions necessary for the evolution of
his own talent. Without it, he is liable to dis-
integrate, to become paranoid, to undervalue the need
to communicate, to waste energy in attacking those
who will not listen, or, even more dramatically, to
commit suicide. All of these negative responses have,
indeed, tended to mark the arts and to disfigure
them since the industrial revolution. But in our
own century the conditions for symbolic creation have
become all but traumatic. According to Leavis the
critical sympathetic and educated community dis-
appeared in England during D.H. Lawrence's life
time. There is not the space - nor is this the context - in which to weigh Leavis' specific judgement.
Here it is important to note the intertwined notion
of cultural continuity and of critical audience.
These I would contend are both central concepts
charting an indispensible area neglected or negated
by the Progressives in English. The life of impulse
- and the life of impulse reflected back to us
through art - requires for its development and
summation, both a bed of inherited culture (the

deeper the better) and an alert, responsive - and
critically responsive - audience (which in the case
of teaching, may, with the right conditions, be provided by the class, the teacher, and, perhaps, even
the school and the immediate community. As we shall
see, the contemporary Sociolinguistic school has
made an important contribution in emphasising the
writer's need for an audience).

What do these principles of cultural continuity and
critical community mean for English teaching? They
point to three responsibilities. Firstly, there is
the responsibility of the English teacher to initiate
the child into the heritage of myth and literature,
to provide the great but uncertain seed of impulse
with a bed of culture, and, heeding the insights of
the Progressives, to do this in intimate relationship to the child's age, needs and creative work.
Secondly, there is the responsibility to slowly convert the class into a critical audience, at once
receptive and discriminating; an audience, it must
be added (extending the narrow Leavisian framework)
not only for the traditional or contemporary writer
'out there', but also for the writer 'within', the
child-writer, the adolescent writer. Thirdly, and
intimately related to the previous responsibilities,
is the English teacher's task to develop an acute
sensitivity to poetic language, to what D.H. Lawrence
called 'arts-speech'. Children should taste on
their tongues the texture of words. In this, a de-
lighting in words and a discriminating between them
should become all but indistinguishable.

To return to Leavis. It can be seen how his great
contribution to English lay in the critical and the
collaborative domain. His strengths resided in:
his awareness of the subleties of language, his
attention to the specific meanings of specific words
in specific texts and contexts, in his appreciation
of the vitality of tradition (including, particularly, that of the English novel and what he established
as the organic line of English poetry), in his insistence on the existential relationship between
literature and human life, in his teaching methods
celebrating the 'third realm' between student and

tutor, <u>between</u> critic and text, that process of
collaboratively establishing tentative meaning in the
act of teaching-and-learning. There were other
strengths too: there was Leavis' courage to oppose
what would seem to be the incurable pathologies of
industrial culture; there was the refusal to compromise within or outside of the University, there was
the refusal to become academic, there was the im-
placcable attack on all the metropolitan organs of
our literary or would-be literary culture. His attack on prevailing orthodoxies and literary coteries
isolated him severely and much of the criticism was
marred by a note of meglomania and paranoia. Yet
the work was necessary. It compelled attention as
surely as it undermined comfort. It exposed the
fifth-rate strutting as the first-rate. It provoked
in the reader an engagement with his own impoverished
yet euphoric age. Above all, it ripped away the pre-
tences of colour-supplement thought and the facade
of liberal publishing houses. Yet, as we shall see,
there were severe limitations to Leavis' position;
before examining them, we must briefly make one more
link between Leavis and the development of English
in our schools.

As is well known, the methods and principles of
Leavis - and of many others who contributed to the
influential <u>Scrutiny</u> (1932 - 1953) - were taken into
English teaching at the secondary level through the
journal <u>The Use of English</u>, founded in 1939 and
edited by Denys Thompson (who had also in 1933
written with Leavis the first text-book on the mass-
media - <u>Culture and Environment</u> and who was later to
be co-founder of the National Association for the
Teaching of English). Through <u>The Use of English</u> and
through the practice of English teachers who had
studied Literature at Downing College, the habits
of critical evaluation of unseen passages, of introducing the best of contemporary literature (at that
time, for example, D.H. Lawrence, T.S. Eliot and
W.B. Yeats),of examining the vacuous rhetoric of
advertising and mass-newspapers became
widespread, particularly in the Grammar Schools. The
seminal energies of the Cambridge School cannot be
seriously denied. The work of David Holbrook (whose

work was to dramatically extend the range of English),
G. H. Bantock, Ian Robinson, Raymond Williams (who was
to take much deeper, and make more complex, Leavis'
sketchy analysis of mass-culture), Richard Hoggart,
Fred Inglis, Frank Whitehead (who after Denys Thompson
was to edit The Use of English), William Walsh, Boris
Ford, the work of all these substantial writers, editors and critics had deep roots in the work of Leavis.
It would be mere journalist patter to offer any sum-
mary of so many authors. I list them as only the
crudest indication of the intellectual and critical
power of the Cambridge School. Their contribution to
a unified concept and detailed practice of English
has been enormous.

What, then, were the flaws, the fatal inadequacies of
conception in the Cambridge School? It was, firstly,
limited in range. It tended to work intensively
within English literature rather than to forge con-
nections with other related traditions. Indeed,
Leavis insisted on virtually defining the whole of
healthy culture as literature; and this is not only
nonsense, but dangerous nonsense, for it negates the
exploration of human experience through art, music,
dance, architecture, and all the other expressive
symbolic terms. Leavis' bias is here even narrower
than Arnold's, and much narrower than Coleridge's.
This contraction of range has had an unfortunate influence in our universities and schools encouraging
English to remain separate from the other expressive
disciplines. English became a well-fortressed island
rather than part of a unified archipelago. The de-
fensive and monolithic attitude to literature served
to keep English arrogantly isolated from the other
complementary expressive arts. In the Grammar
Schools many English Departments became the centres
of critical culture, but for all their excellence,
there was a certain insularity of spirit, a failure
to find the terms necessary for a full aesthetic education, a failure to discern the affinities between
English and Art.

Furthermore there was a marked tendency in the early
Cambridge School to elevate the act of criticism
above the act of creation. The very word 'Scrutiny'
unambiguously proclaimed what kind of activity was

most esteemed. It is, I think, significant that in
his teaching Leavis never asked his students to write
in an imaginative capacity or, even as a means to
comprehend the nature of a particular form or genre.
There was no recognition in his actual pedagogy of
the way in which a student can gain from disciplined
creative work. It is also pertinent to our critique
that Scrutiny published a comparatively small amount
of original poetry and that the only young poet the
journal strongly promoted, Ronald Bottrall, has not,
as his Poems 1955-1973 testify, developed into a
major voice. There was always the danger in the
Cambridge School that criticism, cut off from the
primary experience of artistic creation, would become
dry, inturned, self-perpetuating: critics on critics
on critics .... And there was always the danger of
original insight petrifying into dogma. Too often,
Leavis' personal credo became simply the closed creed
of lesser men (not women, it is interesting to ob-
serve). The circle instead of expanding, contracted.
Did the master himself fall into the trap of wanting
mirrors around him? Had he overlooked the wisdom in
one of Nietzsche's aphorisms which claims that the
good student has to go beyond the teacher, and that
the teacher must urge him to do so?

Dialectically, we are driven back towards the affirm-
ations of the Progressives; back to the need for
creative impulse, alert many-sidedness, authenticity
of naive and stammering response, unfolding inner
process. And, then, we grasp it! The Progressives
and the Cambridge School represent two opposed but
complementary sides of the human psyche, two sides
inerradicably   there and   expressed throughout
Western History in an unending variety of antitheses.
In any reconstitution of English as Art, both sides
must be brought together, into an ever uneasy and
ever creative co-existence. Tradition and creative
impulse, criticism and innovation - these are not
antithetical concepts but complementary, dependent on
each other and defined by each other. We need the
firm arched bow and the flight of the arrow.

Historically it was the work of David Holbrook to
attempt an act of synthesis, to bring together, as it
were, 'the great tradition' and 'the education of the

poetic spirit'. Coming out of the Cambridge School,
studying under Leavis at Downing College, he could
recognise the need for discrimination and critical a-
wareness of the past, but, as a poet and novelist, he
knew also the need to keep symbolism close to the
creative springs of one's own existence, the deep
need in all of us to give order to our confused and
bewildering experience through the elaboration of
phantasy and inward image. His indispensable books
sought to fuse the best of literary criticism with
the best of psychoanalysis. His writing sought to
straddle two fiery traditions and drive them in a
common direction. For over a decade English for
Maturity (1961) and English for the Rejected (1964)
pointed a way forward for English teaching. There is
not space here to evaluate David Holbrook's contribution to English but, without doubt, it has, in the
last few years, been seriously undervalued. From the
perspective of this paper his work, while it did not
adequately define English within the epistemic community of the Arts and while it did not properly emphasise the process of making, or reworking, revising
and shaping in children's writing, yet it did establish the concept of English as an expressive activity.
With great eloquence, marred by a certain diffuseness,
his early works celebrated English as imaginative,
exploratory and aesthetic. But the direction towards
the Arts which David Holbrook's books made possible
again became eclipsed by a further movement, which,
in our search for comprehensive principles, we must
now examine.

5

Certainly the most influential force on English
teaching, during the last fifteen years or so, has
come from what I have already named as the Socio-
Linguistic School, a school which has shown little
appreciation or even knowledge of the Cambridge Movement or the earlier Progressive Movement. This contemporary movement has derived its inspiration less
from Literature or Philosophy, than from Linguistics
and Sociology. After the Newsom Report was published
in 1963, the Sociological Research Unit was funded to

analyse the relationship between language and social
class. The project was directed by Basil Bernstein
and came forward with the volatile notions of the restricted and elaborated codes. More generally the
nature of the work encouraged a new interest in
spoken language, (revealed, for example, in Douglas
Barnes' and James Britton's writings), an element
which both the Progressives and Cambridge School had
largely ignored. The London Institute of Education
with its sociological research into language and with
its own PGCE course run by Harold Rosen, became both
physically and symbolically one of the centres for
the new English. The other centre was provided by
the Nuffield Programme in Linguistics and English
Teaching, directed from 1964 to 1970 by M.A.K. Halliday. The project, having a more direct influence on
English teaching than Bernstein's research, culminated in Language in Use (1968) encouraging an analytical study of different forms of language, a text now
found in many classrooms. It is not without significance that both these projects were given an offical
imprimatur by the Bullock Report (1975) for in many
ways the projects provide the ideological background
to that massive document.

The great virtue of the Socio-Linguistic School was
that it looked broadly at language and understood it
as a formative energy of the mind seeking order and
pattern. It saw language as crucial to the whole
curriculum and gave a new significance to oracy, to
the activity of speaking, to the daily personal making of meaning and order through informal discussion
and immediate conversation. 'The spoken language in
England', wrote Andrew Wilkinson, 'has been shamefully neglected. Oracy is central'. Unlike, for example, Arnold and Sampson in the literary tradition,
the Sociologists realized that there were many forms
- idioms, registers, codes - of language, all, in
their own context, appropriate and valuable. Halliday, on dialect and idiom, is eloquent:

> A speaker who is made ashamed of his
> own language habits suffers a basic
> injury as a human being: to make any-
> one, especially a child, feel so a-
> shamed is as indefensible as to make

him feel ashamed of the colour of his
skin.

Dialect, where it exists, it was argued, is not a
corruption of English but a distinct expression of it
as valid, because it exists and is used, as any other
form. In their respect for the variety of language,
the Socio-Linguistic writers express a deeper conception of the complex nature of language than George
Sampson and Matthew Arnold with their misconceived
and imperialistic desire 'to set the standard of
speech for the Empire'. It has been the distinct a-
chievement of Bernstein, Barnes, Britton and Halliday
to heighten _every_ teacher's awareness of language by
making him highly attentive to the different types of
speech used by children in the classroom. The imperative 'Language across the curriculum' was the inevitable outcome.

The Sociolinguists' contribution to education has, in
its own way, been as distinct as that of the earlier
traditions of English. As with the traditions we
have already described so with the Sociolinguists:
they have provoked, shocked, and deeply challenged
entrenched views, blowing to the wind the innumerable
husks of dead practice. With their broad concern for
'language' and 'communication', they were able to
cast a dazzling beam of light onto the mundane realities of so much teaching in this country. Against
the reluctant acquisition of scattered information,
which then passes for teaching and learning, the
linguists asserted the primacy of process and the
need for expressive language, that language through
which each pupil personally makes sense of the facts
and begins to grasp for himself the principles behind
them. In massive attempts to clarify its own preoccupations with language and learning, the Sociolinguists hammered out fresh conceptual schemata
which served to further expose the pedagogic confusion of our schools. At another level, their work
constituted a critique of traditional positivist ep-
istemology. Tne Sociolinguists wanted to demonstrate
that truth was not simply 'out there' to be merely
imprinted on the passive mind of the child; but that
it was made through individual attempts to actively
formulate meaning. That, therefore, truth could only

be found through the personal tussle to find words,
symbols, representative forms. It followed that a
school which did not allow the pupil space to formulate his own responses, thoughts, conceptions, des-
troyed the very premise on which any meaningful sense
of education must stand. One particular merit of the
Sociolinguistic movement has been its ability to keep
principle and practice, abstract theory and tangible
implication closely tethered. It has also had the
courage to stand by its conclusions.

One schemata elaborated by the Sociolinguists was the
now too familiar 'Transactional-Expressive-Poetic'
division of language. Whatever objections may be
brought against the classification (and the theory)
it was richly productive and remains a useful tool.
The following charts, for example, taken from Writing
and Learning across the Curriculum (1975) record, in
a devastating manner, the amount of futile 'learning'
which takes place in our secondary schools. In its
abstract form it is as telling to our Reason as
Dicken's Hard Times is telling to our Imagination,
and it is telling the same truth: facts, facts,
facts.

Kinds of writing across the Secondary Curriculum

	Year 1	Year 3	Year 5	Year 7
Transactional	54	57	62	84
Expressive	6	6	5	4
Poetic	17	23	24	7
Miscellaneous	23	14	9	5

Function by subject

	English	History	Geography	RE	Science
Transactional	34	88	88	57	92
Expressive	11	0	0	11	0
Poetic	39	2	0	12	0
Miscellaneous	26	10	12	20	8

It would take a whole volume or a month of seminars
to draw out the full implications of these two
charts. I reprint them here only as an example of
the power of the linguist's schemata to illuminate
practice   and as an example of the kind of evidence marshalled to testify to the Sociolinguist's
indictment of much teaching and learning. The dia-
gram makes abundantly clear why a shift from Literature to Language took place, why it may even have
been necessary and why the movement had to be, be-
neath the garbs of academic study and the classification of data, valuably subversive and engaged.

Yet the Socio-Linguistic school ultimately left the
English teacher in a highly ambiguous position, an
eagle stretched across the curriculum but without
nest or offspring. All the research and all the
writing revealed infinitely more about English as a
medium (my second definition) than English as a discipline (my third definition). It contributed virtually nothing to the study of literature nor to the
development of creative work i.e. work, in their
terms, moving from the expressive into the poetic
category. In fact, although we shall move on to examine what happened to English, it is doubtful
whether the Sociolinguists really believed in English
as a unique discipline, with its own field and distinct pedagogy. Past formulations were cut away as
if they had never been. Overnight, in the theory at
least, English became either a sort of Linguistics or
a sort of Social Studies. Had there ever been other
approaches? Had one asked such a tactless question,
one might have heard the reply 'Leavis? Ah! - an
elitist' or 'Holbrook? Marjorie Hourde? Lost in the
(bourgeois) vagaries of Psycho-analysis'.

Two distinct approaches emerged as possible answers
to the fundamental question 'What is the discipline
of English?' The first approach was to make English
mean Linguistics. We have already had occasion to
mention Language in Use. The Bullock Report described
this textbook as follows:

> The principle of the programme is to
> some extent like that of geographical
> and botanical field work, in that it

involves studying specimens of language.

Language in Use attempted to turn English into a
linguistic science, a cognitive, essentially neutral,
introduction to linguistic forms. In the light of
our argument so far, such a substitution has to be
sharply queried. Certainly such a text might be
quite indispensable to the study of linguistics as
an optional fifth form or sixth form course. What
it cannot be is an adequate substitute for the discipline of English as it has built up over the last
eighty years, with its commitment to the cultural
heritage and to the emotional development of the individual through the agency of the creative word.
Linguistics is a specialised analytical study of
language in all its variety; English as a discipline
is the cultivation of one specific form of language:
language charged with feeling and personality, the
language of the individual (whether pupil or mature
writer) moved by the power of feeling or compelled
by the unifying force of imagination. English is
practical and expressive: Linguistics is theoretical
and scientific. The disciplines have language in
common, but their methods and aims are, for most of
the time, quite different.

Another way of expressing our opposition to Linguistics in this specific context is to say that English is
centrally concerned with the making and appreciation
of Literature. Yet, literature, in many of the arguments for Linguistics, was reduced to being little
more than just another manifestation of language, a
manifestation that was even dying out, that was, perhaps, in no way essential to the functioning of materialist civilization. Peter Doughty, in characteristic vein, declared that the new English teacher
should be committed to 'language in all its complexity and variety and not merely the highly idiosyncratic form of literature'. The highly idiosyncratic
form of Homer, Shakespear and D.H. Lawrence! Halliday, in the same light or, more truly, in the same
darkness, insisted that the true discipline for the
English teacher was no longer Literature - that idiosyncratic version of language destined to die out in
the TV metropolis - but Linguistics. It was as if
F.R. Leavis and David Holbrook and countless others

had never lifted their pens. Earlier traditions of
English teaching had been, with alarming efficiency,
simply erased. In the numb space buzzed the small
insects 'communications', 'skills', 'strategies',
'language operates', the drone of a new technicism.
Curiously, as the word 'communication' fell like lead
from the lips of a million teachers, so there seemed
less and less to say. What had been overlooked in
the pathological obsession for communications was the
elusive underground of the psyche, those preconcept-
ual sources of latent formulation locked in the emergent impulses of the body and the unconscious. Only
by maintaining contact with these deeper pre-verbal
energies can language itself remain resonant,
charged, rich, strange, compelling and worthwhile.
Creativity exists prior to words. And words, if they
are to have the power of authentic utterance, must
return constantly to their non-verbal origins, back
to the creative impulse. The rejection of psychoanalysis had, indeed, been premature. Without any
sense of depth or inner mystery, 'communications' was
destined to become confined to surfaces, growing ever
thinner, ever more transparent until there was nothing left to say, except words.

The second approach has been to take English in the
direction of Social Studies, into the explicit and
continuous discussion (theoretically 'neutral', although in fact often slanted ideologically to the
Left) of social and moral issues. The themes were
generally presented through literary, and not so literary, extracts. The most well known example of this
approach was Lawrence Stenhouse's Humanities Project
(1978) with its 'relevant' material (on the family,
on war, etc) with its insistence on the teacher as
'neutral chairman' and its goal of 'tolerance'.

There was nothing particularly new in the Humanities
Project. As early as 1963 in the textbook Reflect-
ions there had been a marked shift in English towards
the discussion of social issues through the reading
of extracts from a largely contemporary literature.
At the time in the early Sixties the approach seemed
convincing and, without doubt, it encouraged some
excellent work in the classroom, particularly in the
socially-mixed classrooms of the new Comprehensives.

But after a decade or so, with the publication of innumerable anthologies parading the nightmares of
pollution, abortion, unemployment, racial segrega-
tion, teacher and parent cruelty, strikes, women's
liberation, prostitution, homosexuality, alcoholism,
drug addiction, capitalist exploitation, children's
rights, nuclear war, suicide and the futility of the
educational system, the approach became - how shall
we say it? - sordidly nihilistic.

From the point of view of this essay however, a more
important objection has to be recorded about this
kind of work being done under the umbrella of English
for its proper epistemological roots lie not in
English but in Sociology and Ethics. If literature
is employed solely to spark off a discussion of
'issues', moving ever away from the metaphor to the
abstraction, then imaginative texts are being roughly
abused. They are not being conveyed, but betrayed.
There is little doubt in my mind that during the last
fifteen years, under the influence of the Sociolinguistic School, much literature has been betrayed in
our classroom, twisted from high imaginative art into
quick ideological stimulus. The logical direction of
such a method has taken English, in many of our
schools, into common Humanity courses. In such/an alli-
ance English tends to lose that unique mode of imaginative and emotional indwelling in literature where
one is not irritably seeking out social issues for
rational debate, but, rather, trying to identify and
grow with newly felt emergent experience. We politi-
cize literature at the cost of authenticity. Again,
it is a matter of renewing faith in forces which
transcend the merely given, of allowing art its own
underground logic and, yes, its own kind of hidden
'praxis'.

One further and intimately related objection must be
recorded. There is, among the Sociolinguists I have
rather brutally caged together, a certain predilec-
tion to convert intellectual disciplines into ideological constructions. In the writing of Harold
Rosen and Chris Searle we cannot but discern, a com-
pulsive identification of English with the oppressed
members of our society - with the immigrants, the
unemployed, the proletariat - which, while it draws

heavily on our desires for social justice, yet in an
educational context becomes out of place and danger-
ously exclusive. In its worst forms it is Philistine,
sentimental, mindless, and highly destructive. It
would dismiss the whole of English literature as
bourgeouis culture and, without any qualification or
unease, erect the razmatazz of the slum-street into
the only form of authentic existence. Analysing the
position of Chris Searle, Sonia Courtnadge (1980)
has written:

> "Although Searle criticises middle class
> society as one which thrives on divi-
> sions, I would argue what he is doing
> is equally divisive. The approach is
> one which seeks to insulate the child
> within his own environment and 'class',
> for, in order to achieve working class
> solidarity, the pupils are urged to
> eschew all 'middle class' language and
> literature and 'to see his own life in
> terms of his immediate surroundings,
> his own world'. He will gain his know-
> ledge from his neighbours and environ-
> ment, not from a different conscious-
> ness at school".

At its best, education must spring from a universal-
ity of principle, it must strive to be comprehensive
rather than partial and should seek to feed that deep
human impulse for transcendence. It must avoid bol-
stering all comfortable enclosing presuppositions,
inertly inherited; it does not matter where the
presuppositions come from, from the country house,
from the suburban semi-detached or the slum-dwelling.
Education is a fearless enquiry into human meaning
and an energy for diverse authentic growth, it is not
a pre-selected political struggle. It is an act of
making whose outcome cannot be told until the last
poem is written and the last theory hypothesised.
Perhaps the Sociolinguists have been guilty of trying
to close the very process which they had worked so
diligently to make open and porous? And this, as is
so often the case, with the best of political intentions, the finest of moral convictions.

I have implied that the concept of English as a medium
across the curriculum has been the major contribution
of the Sociolinguists. I wish to draw this element
in particular from the work of the Institute and The
Bullock Report because it provides one of the necessary conditions for the autonomy of English as a lit-
erary-expressive discipline. But, here at least we
find a continuity. In 1975 James Britton in introducing Writing and Learning Across the Curriculum had
written:

> "One of the most far-reaching changes
> in education envisaged by the Bullock
> Committee is to be found in its
> recommendation that all teachers
> should seek to foster learning in
> their particular areas by taking re-
> sponsibility for the language develop-
> ment of their students in that area."

'Far-reaching' it no doubt was. And yet in 1920, 55
years before, in English for the English George Sampson had anticipated the same principle:

> ".... no teachers, whether of sciences,
> or languages or mathematics, or history
> or geography must be allowed to evade
> their own heavy responsibilities. They
> must not say 'Our business is to teach
> Science or Mathematics or French, not
> English'. That is the great fallacy of
> 'subject' teaching. It is very defin-
> itely their business to teach English;
> and their failure to recognise it as
> their business is a cause of the evil
> they deplore. In a sense the function
> of history, geography, science and so
> forth in school is to provide material
> for the teaching of English. The
> specialist teacher defeats his own
> purpose precisely to the extent to
> which he neglects the language of his
> pupils'.

In the notion of language across the curriculum, we
find a further tenet necessary for the reconstruction

of English as Art. If all teachers are rightfully
concerned with the development of language as it relates to their own particular subject then English as
a discipline is released to occupy its own place in
the curriculum. Ironically, what that place is has
been badly obscured by those very arguments which established the principle. But in this analysis we have
grown accustomed to the necessary partiality of evolv-
ing ideas; to one truth blotting out another to establish itself and then in establishing itself to reveal its inadequacies. Ideas and movements grow
dialectically and require, in turn, a dialectical
approach. What is omitted is as crucial as what is
asserted. And this being the case we who would
understand and, in turn, restructure, must work
obliquely and underground as well as across surfaces
and directly. What we begin to see emerging out of
the traditions (and how soon innovation becomes tradition! - another dialectical paradox) is yet a
further shape to English, which incorporates within
the best of the past, and yet remains new in its more
comprehensive pattern and still awaits its full formation, its necessary practice.

6.

My analysis of all three traditions has been highly
condensed and highly schematic (doing no justice to
any of the individuals I have either quoted or list-
ed). As I said at the outset my account is not a
neutral one, not a historian's account, not an
account for posterity. Rather it is an analysis provoked by a feeling of disquiet about the existing
state of English, since, say, the time of The Bullock
Report. Certainly by the beginning of the 80s I felt
that English had become impossibly diffuse in its interests, too eclectic in its approaches and too
narrowly political in many of its formulations. At
the same time, there was the miserable knowledge that
in many classrooms across the country there had been
an appalling reversion to habits which had been con-
demned as early as 1920, those old habits for example
of grammatical dissection and the filling in of
blanks inserted into, otherwise, impeccably dull

sentences. English Departments, quite simply, had
lost direction and faced a dismal future in which
they might cease to exist except as 'Communications'
or 'Skills Laboratories' serving the other established disciplines. Above all, as I said in my introduction, English had neglected the aesthetic realm,
leaving the curriculum pathologically biased towards
the cognitive.

The condition has provoked the analysis. I am only
too aware of its inadequacies, its stridency of tone,
its tendency to polemic, its inability to establish
the decent qualification. And yet it must stand, as
a preliminary attempt to work towards a full definition of English within the wider category of Art.
In this respect I have found the most convincing work
on English as a Discipline during the last decade to
be the Schools Council Project on the Arts, in Robert
Witkin's The Intelligence of Feeling, and in Malcolm
Ross' The Arts and the Adolescent and The Creative
Arts. These publications, I believe, struggle to
provide a conceptual framework in which English, as
an expressive discipline, could begin to thrive. To
their work, we should bring, experimentally, the
principles I have extracted from the three traditions
of English teaching:

> From the Progressives, the emphasis on
> impulse and the innate tendency towards
> individuation.

> From the Cambridge School, the emphasis
> on tradition, discrimination and critical
> audience.

> From the Sociolinguists the emphasis on
> process and the clarifying principle of
> 'Language across the Curriculum'.

The implications of such a reconstitution of English
could be quite revolutionary. For the first time in
this country English would be drawn into the circle
of the other, much neglected, expressive disciplines.
New forms of collaboration would emerge from this encounter (the skilled printing and illustrating of
prose and poetry, the setting of original songs to

music, common Arts Festivals in the schools, the dramatic improvisation of myth and fable etc.). Such collaborations and joint productions would encourage vigorous thinking about the nature of creativity and, perhaps, begin to illuminate that dark area we designate 'affective' - and then forget - in our academic books on education. And, almost of necessity, such awareness would lead to an arts programme which would demand what it has never had in state education, a fitting share of the curriculum, about one third rather than, as at present, one tenth of the whole.

The arts form on indispensable symbolic form for the integration of experience. If in this country we are to talk of a core curriculum then we must include, without ambiguity or hesitation, the Arts. What we now need to hear on the lips of teachers and parents is not so much the cry 'English (as a medium) across the curriculum' although that is still necessary. What is more urgent is the cry 'English (as a discipline) within the Arts' and, finally, 'The Arts within a total curriculum'. I have written this paper to that end.

REFERENCES

Courtnadge, S. (1980), A Conceptual and Autobiographical Enquiry into the Present State of English Teaching. M.A. Dissertation for the University of Sussex, 1980.

Halliday, M. (1964), The Linguistic Sciences and Language Teaching. Longman.

Leavis, F.R. (1975), The Living Principle. Chatto and Windus.

Martin, N. (1976), Writing and Learning Across the Curriculum. Ward Lock Educational.

Read, H. (1943), Education Through Art. Faber and Faber.

Sampson, G. (1921), English for the English. Cambridge.

The Relevance of Art in Education

VICTOR HEYFRON

"If people were free, then art would be
the form and expression of their
freedom". Herbert Marcuse (1979).
'The Aesthetic Dimension'.

What precisely are policy makers demanding when they
claim that the curriculum should be relevant? Is the
sense in which they are urging relevance one in which
aesthetic education easily fits? Jerome Bruner (1971)
makes a distinction between personal and social relevance. Personal relevance refers to those experi
ences which are immediate, self-regarding and meaningful, and social relevance refers to knowledge
which leads to the solution of the 'grievous problems
facing the world'. Whilst not altogether disregard-
ing personal relevance, he argues strongly that those
subjects, namely, the sciences, which contribute to
the solution of practical problems, should form the
basis of the curriculum. In times of scarcity, when
people's lives are dominated by the material concerns
of earning a living, it is easy to view relevance in
the curriculum as one of pragmatic instrumentality.
In this kind of context art is typically considered a
luxury and superfluous to the real business of living. The notion that art is a luxury is fostered by
the view that art is autonomous and that justifications for its pursuit should not incorporate extra
aesthetic dimensions but should refer exclusively to
aesthetic properties. Typically this view, mirroring
Eisner's notion of essentialistic justifications, is
characterized as 'art for its own sake'. I shall
attempt to clear a pathway between these two extremes
by suggesting that art is relevant to the lives of

children and society in both the personal existential
sense and the social, and that claims that it is not
are founded on a mistaken notion of the way art gets
its value. For the question 'What is the relevance
of art?' posed by the pragmatist suggest justifications
in terms other than those that characterize the aesthetic, e.g. in terms of mental hygiene, technolog-
ical advancement, and economic welfare. Whereas an
examination of the nature of value in art will reveal that rather than providing solutions to specific
practical problems it enters into our consciousness
of a social existence categorically different, but
nevertheless significant, way. There is an interlock
between fundamental humanizing projects and the aesthetic. In brief, engagement in the aesthetic is instrumental to a person becoming conscious of himself
(and man) as possessing intrinsic worth, and in virtue of which aesthetic education is relevant to the
child growing up in an industrial society.

However, whether or not a person initiated into the
realm of the arts will as a matter of fact act more
effectively in the wider context of living is a topic
for empirical research. There are numerous putative
justifications of art based on the assumption that,
say, perceptual discrimination, imagination and political awareness, social understanding, and openness
of judgement will transfer from artistic to non-
artistic situations. Malcolm Ross (1980) in 'The
Predicament of the Arts' warns us not to place too
much weight on these types of arguments. We must
look to the evidence mustered in the literature to
authenticate these claims. My argument rests on logical rather than psychological premises. The thesis
of my argument is that engagement in the arts necessarily exhibits a potentiality we cannot not value,
namely, the freedom to envisage preferred versions of
humanity. This value is made manifest in the act of
creating or appreciating. It is obvious that art is
only one of a number of activities which promotes a
child's sense of worth, but its relevance for the
curriculum is justified in the particular way it
picks out and reflects the individual's unique perspective on the world. This matters in the context
of his art work, it is a criterion of merit in a way
that it is not in other areas of the curriculum.

AI - J

Nevertheless, there are general criteria embodied in
the tradition of art in virtue of which he shares a
mind with others, and which not only can he not ignore, but are a condition of his creative or appreciative activities. It is in relation to this condition that the art educator has a particular responsibility, namely to encourage the pupil to articulate his being through art in increasing qualitative
complexity.

Before expanding on this last claim, I want to say
more about the notion of relevance, especially in
connection with Bruner's point that relevance directs
us to 'goals we care about'. An examination of the
concept of relevance reveals that that which is considered relevant contextually is dependent for its
value on some other state of affairs, that is, it
presupposes a means-end relationship. For example, a
a relevant piece of information is one which contributes to the solution of a problem someone wants to
solve. A skill is irrelevant if it fails to meet
someone's purposes, in spite of any inherently valuable features it may possess. In brief, that which
is relevant is that which is judged to be instrumental to individual or social purposes. The notion of
relevance fits in more readily with instrumental
justifications of educational provision than 'intrinsic justifications'. However, claims about the relevance of an activity are empty without reference to a
context in which the 'goals people care about' are
manifest. For example, in a context of economic de-
pression a curriculum may endorse activities which
maximize opportunities for getting jobs and passing
examinations, whereas in a context in which character
building is esteemed an entirely different range of
activities is encouraged. It follows from this that
debates about the relevance of a curriculum are dependent upon the particular ends to which schooling
is seen as a means. They involve on the one hand
technical agreements about the efficiency of the
means prescribed for some determinate end, and, on
the other, ethical and prudential agreements about
the desirability of achieving these ends. These ends
are contingent on the particular ends people care
about.

Conceptual arguments which support prescriptions
about the ends of education, such as pursuing knowledge for its own sake, depend on conceptual truths,
and are not subject to the same type of rebut as
those which prescribe the desirability of providing
skilled manpower for industry, and hence are not to be
formally opposed by reference to contingent purposes
people may happen to have. The implications of so
doing, for example, may lead parents to refuse to
value art education, or at least to accept its relevance on the school curriculum.

Debates about the curriculum are complex, they are
essentially about priorities and balance, and if the
art educator is to convince the materialist that art
should figure prominently on the curriculum, his
arguments should be directed towards ends which embody conceptions of man which it would be difficult
for a person who cares about democratic processes not
to accept as valid. The problem would be not that of
convincing the materialist that the particular ends
are worthwhile, but rather that the means are effective towards these ends, for example, that initiation
into the arts is instrumental to a person coming to
see   his individual perspective on life as significant. There is a sense in which appealing to a
person's conception of something is important to
establishing the fact of that conception. For example, the fact that my conception of a person is one
which includes the notion that people are deserving
of respect is a condition of treating them with respect, and, consequently, of them believing that they
are respected.

Correspondingly, the fact that a child comes to believe on appropriate grounds that he has personal
worth is a condition of him having personal worth.
Having convinced the materialist that his conception
of man includes the notion of autonomy as a distinguishing characteristic, and that people on
appropriate grounds should respect themselves and
others as having personal worth, we have to show that
the aesthetic is a means to this end. I am not
speaking here of a mistaken virtuosity, or a cultural
enrichment which ignores other dimensions of human
experience, which is itself a form of impoverishment,

but rather a fundamental impoverishment that the
failure to transcend the facticity of practical reality would entail, namely, the inability to assert,
and thus realize, the freedom and imagination pre-
supposed by the recognition of our potentiality for
envisaging alternative versions of humanity. Herbert
Marcuse makes a similar point when he writes:

hve a read quote

> "Art breaks open a dimension inassess-
> ible to other experience, a dimension
> in which human beings, nature and
> things no longer stand under the law
> of established reality."
> (The Aesthetic Dimension, p.72, 1979).

So far, I have suggested that art is not to be justified, in an educational context in which it is recommended that all children receive a substantial
initiation into the arts, solely as an end in itself
without reference to extra artistic features, or
solely as a means along with a number of other means
to some specific end. For in the first case, there
is the possibility of genuine disagreement about the
desirability of pursuing art (e.g. a person may prefer sport!) and in the second case, there may be a
more efficient means to the proposed end. In the
case in which the end presupposes artistic skill
(e.g. designing artifacts, cultivating an environment), art is limited to a specialized function in
society with the possibility of calling in the
'expert'; in which case even though it is highly desirable that some children receive an art education,
it is unnecessary for all children to gain the
appropriate expertise. The kind of justification I
have suggested is one in which art is seen as
specially instrumental to an end which it is difficult to conceive that even the educational pragmatist
is not committed, namely, that on appropriate grounds
children in developing the capacity to attach meaning
and significance to their lives come to see themselves (and others) as having worth. That children
should come to care about such a goal, and that we
should live in a society in which people attach meaning and significance to their lives, is beyond dis-
pute; but, that engagement in the arts is the special means by which this capacity is realized still

needs to be argued.

What then is the special sense in which the arts are
relevant to a person's life? To what extent does the
lack of a capacity to appreciate nature and works of
art, and to express feelings in an art medium lead to
an impoverishment of a person's being? There is an
obvious sense in which we can say that without an
initiation into the arts a person will be unable to
appreciate aesthetic objects or express his feelings
in an art medium, and as a matter of fact we believe
that these are worthwhile ends to pursue. The extent that we believe an inadequate initiation will
lead to an impoverishment of a person's life will depend upon our beliefs about the nature or purpose of
art. We may believe that the way art contributes to
a person's life parallels that of other subjects and
activities, e.g. sport and mathematics. But I want
to argue that art as art enters into the weave of
life in a more fundamental way than many other activities on the curriculum. That is, it is a special
way of sensitively apprehending and caring about our
lives. It is a distinctively humanizing process.
Other activities and circumstances may indirectly enhance or diminish our sense of worth whilst in pursuit of standard ends, but art, through the sensuous
embodiment of its subject matter, directly engages
the individual in apprehending the human condition as
significant.

In order to make sense of the notion that art is instrumental to the individual apprehending his life as
significant, it will be useful to consider the way in
which perceiving ordinary objects and engaging in
non-artistic activities give pleasure. The patterning of features of an activity give pleasure to the
extent they signify desirable aspects of our being.
They are criteria against which we evaluate our personal worth. For example, doing the washing up reveals I am socially approved, serving into the tennis
netting that I lack competence, rescuing the child
from a burning house that I am courageous. In a similar way objects record the traces of an activity and
display that which we value, for example, the shine
on the shoe, the blot on the paper. These pursuits
and objects have standard ends which are separately

identifiable from, but quite consistent with, that of
conferring worth on our person, i.e. they are logically but not existentially separable from fundamental
purposes constitutive of being a person. For example,
whilst having a job is a means of securing basic material ends, it also confers worth on us as persons.
The knowledge I have a job confirms aspects of my being which if I evaluate positively enhances my sense
of worth. This worth is inextricably linked to public and personal conceptions of what it is to be a
worthwhile citizen or human being. Typically, engagement in these activities embody a person as an
approved agent. This embodiment is a condition of
identifying and individuating his personal existence.
The external representation of our being in objects
and activities approximate to the aesthetic to the
extent that they enable us to identify with, and project, valued states. They differ from the aesthetic
to the extent that these valued states do not depend
for their significance on the distinctive marks of
the maker. In creating a work of art, the artist intends his marks to be noticed both as significant and
as his marks.

The following schematic outline of the existential
view that man is a being whose being is an issue for
him will help to support the assertion that man is
prone to see valued aspects of himself (and others)
in what he does and in his surroundings, and in virtue of which he is able to articulate his being.
Sartre argues in 'Being and Nothingness', for example,
that man as a being with consciousness has no fixed
nature and must create his own being. He argues that
man, unlike physical objects, cannot be defined ex-
haustively in terms of a priori properties, for it is
always possible for him to respond to his situation
in the light of purposes to which he has freely committed himself. Unless we know a man's specific purposes we cannot predict his response to his environment in the way science predicts the outcome of environmental forces on inanimate objects. However, a
condition of man's freedom to devise his own purposes
and that of detaching himself from the causal sequence of events that make up the phenomenal world,
is a constant lack in his being. This lack phenomen-
ologically reveals itself as a form of fundamental

anxiety, and as a yearning to become 'thinglike'. In
this state any characterization seems psychologically
preferable to total anonymity, even if becoming
'something' rather than 'nothing' makes us dependent
on the evaluations of others. There is a close connection between identifying individuating properties
and attaching significance to them in respect of this
identification. In one way or another, intentionally
drawing attention to a feature is saying that it
matters, i.e. the identification presupposes a purpose. Since others are distinct centres of consciousness and are able to formulate and attach significance to their purposes, they potentially confirm
aspects of our being by attributing certain characteristics to us, but this may be done irrespective of
whether the bearer genuinely believes the characterization is an authentic one. One way, then, of
apprehending our being and attaching derivative worth
to our personal existence is by intentionally conforming to the expectations of significant others, a
consequence of which is that the form of our being is
fixed by another. Individual dimensions of our being
have worth then only insofar as they fit in with the
purposes of, and are noted by, this other person.
Whereas, in the context of art, the freedom to formulate purposes distinctive of our being is inseparable from creative and appreciative activitites.
There is a sense in which the social world is the
ground of our being; and in which identification with
the characterizations of others, which we believe
authentically marry with our own evaluations of what
is worthwhile, have integrity. However, we may conform with characterizations purely because they are
approved and not for any other reason. There is a
danger that if we disregard our own purposes and reg-
ulate our lives solely by reference to other people's
purposes we will alienate ourselves from our surroundings. Importantly, we will fail to assert the
creative dimension of our existence by refusing to
formulate and to give significance to aspects of our
being which reflect our vital purposes.

Apprehending our being authentically then, is not a
matter of deducing characteristics from a priori
principles or constructing a public manner from a set
of social norms, it is analogous to the way we

confirm the existence of physical objects in the phenomenal world by reference to sense experience. That
is, it is immediate. It is not an inference from a
set of properties. We recognize and confirm our purposes and what we are in what we do, a paradigm case
of which is the way we confirm our moral worth in our
acts. It is one thing, for example, to believe we
are courageous because our friends tell us we are or
because of certain fantasies we have about ourselves,
but quite another to confirm our courage in circumstances which call for us to act in ways we believe
courageous people ought to act. We accept our response to a situation as one criterion of what we
are. So, if we run away from a dangerous situation
whilst believing we ought to remain, we have no
grounds on which to claim we are courageous. The
features of the situation 'stand for' this lack of
worth. We stand accused by our actions. A non-
artistic example will help to make this point clearer. Imagine a mountaineer reaching the top of a difficult cliff. He looks down and savours the particular rocks he has just climbed. He notes with particular pleasure the difficult overhangs and ridges;
they exhibit to him his skill and courage. The
awareness of these features is enjoyable, they 'stand
for' characteristics which he fundamentally values.
Correspondingly, I want to argue that the sensuous
elements of a painting or piece of music embody purposes of the artist and exhibit the world as meaningful, and absorbtion in the looking is a mark of this
consciousness. Adrian Stokes (1963) echoes this view
when he writes

> "the inner world forces its imprint of
> a symbol upon all perception; but art
> devotes itself entirely to sense data,
> to every significance attaching to
> them, in order to focus steadily on
> integration of the inner world as an
> outer image."
> (Painting and the Inner World, p.4).

We find traces of ourselves in the world in a variety
of ways and the significance we attach to these marks
depends upon the extent they enhance our sense of
worth. The ordinary everyday activities in which most

of us are engaged are regulated by the practical
purposes that make up our lives e.g. securing basic
material ends, maintaining social relations, servicing the car, canvassing for a political party. Fig-
uratively, we get into the world through our acts and
the objects that we make, and our worth is publically
confirmed. There is a sense in which the features of
our acts carry with them our personal style and hence
assert our individuality but the relationship between
the performance of a social role and the extent it
uniquely characterizes an individual is restricted on
logical grounds by the end to which it is a means.
That is, the patterning of the features of an act is
regulated by the end towards which it is directed.
In art, in contrast, the distinctive pattern of the
work is itself a criterion of merit. It is this criterion which marks off artistic activities from non-
artistic activities, at least, insofar as they do not
approximate to the aesthetic. Through the work of
art the spectator is able to experience a unique patterning of elements which constitute the individual
perspective of the artist.

We need now to consider in more detail the way in
which art gains its significance. This is especially
important if we are to provide an adequate account of
the relevance of art in education. The following im-
pressionistic account, although schematic, is sufficiently broad in outline to suggest an approach to
this problem. In the example of the climber, the
pleasure the mountaineer received from contemplating
his mountainous route depended upon the signifiance
he attached to possessing climbing skills and acting
courageously. In a parallel way, we need to consider
the basis of the enjoyment in a work of art. For example, what valued ends do the marks of a painting
confirm? And what is the nature of the relationship
between the features of a work and its subject matter.
I have argued above that the value of art is not to
be characterized solely in terms of its intrinsic
qualities, or justified by reference to specific material ends to which it is a means: it is to be justified in terms of conferring significance on a person's individual perspective.

There is a close connection between the impact a work

has on us and the significance we attach to it. The
intensity of the sensuous impression both corollates
with, and registers the extent of, this significance.
The sensuous resists and melds with consciousness.
The sensuous in art is especially relevant to art education. It directly engages children and exhibits
to them what it means to value something for its own
sake, e.g. colours, sounds, textures, movement, all
make an immediate impact on the senses. However,
art's significance does not lie merely in the
pleasure that the patterning of sensuous qualities
affords. The profundity we attach to works of art
goes beyond the mere presentation of its phenomenal
properties toward some form of symbolic embodiment.
For example, it matters that it is the bird who sings
his song and not a human imitator (Kant (1951)).
And in the same way, it matters that the artist as
such does not merely copy the paintings of another
artist. In the first case, we cease to appreciate
the bird's song when we discover that it is an imitation. Although the sensuous qualities of the
imitator's rendition are indistinguishable from a
bird's song, because I know it is not the bird's I do
not find it aesthetically pleasing. Intuitively,
this suggests that the sensuous patterning in itself
is not sufficient for the aesthetic, something else
needs to be present. Consider the following speculative account as a candidate for what the bird's
song is about. The patterning of the sensuous tones
of the bird's song symbolises an existence which is
not bound by human preoccupations. There is pleasure
in contemplating the wildness and freedom in nature
which the bird's song connotes, e.g. we hear a bird-
singing-in-nature rather than merely a patterning of
sensuous notes. Freedom and wildness infuse the sensuous, and the patterning of the notes 'stand for'
these states. It transports us in imagination away
from the practical reality of our mundane purposes.
The bird symbolises a way of existing 'as-free'. The
sensuous patterning of notes enable us to identify
with the song and symbolically get into the world.
That we are aware of something like these meanings
infusing the sensuous is suggested by our refusal to
allow the imitator's song serious aesthetic consideration. The sensuous is a necessary but not a sufficient condition for aesthetic significance. In the

second case, insofar as we recognise that a painting
is a copy of another painting we know that the
features of the painting are not traces of a creative
activity. There is no internal relationship between
the patterning of sensuous marks and the conscious
activity of the artist striving to give form to content in a medium. Important subject matter is
neither a necessary or sufficient condition for attributing significance to a work of art. For within
the context of art the medium draws attention to its
content as significant. For example, imagine an artist preoccupied with a supposedly trivial concern
e.g. Fragonard's depiction of leisurely romps. We
may criticise him as a person occupying his time in
depicting trivia, but we applaud his artistry in
making trivia appear significant. In the context of
art the subject matter is irrelevant as such, for example, even boredom and futility in art are presented
as significant. Within the context of art life is
given significance rather than the other way round.
It is in the creating and appreciating of the sensuous patterning of form that the potentiality to
transform our mode of existence is realized. It reveals the possibility of an imaginative disengagement
from our practical concerns, vivifying the present
and endorsing our subjectivity. Works of art are the
outer articulation of inner processes and both inner
and outer are made intelligible by reference to one
another. The apprehension of an inner life is made
possible by the determinate traces in an art object
which registers these processes. It is the recognition of these traces as distinctive features of our
inner life and our potentiality to transcend the mundane that gives significance to art. To the extent
that engagement in the arts is something we do, it
reveals purposes to which we are committed, the form
of which is freely chosen and given significance in a
summation of sensuous gestures which are the traces
of the mind which conceived them. We attach significance to them, if we do, because they reveal to us
that which we fundamentally value, namely, the freedom to conceive of potential modes of existing to
which we can commit ourselves. For example, identification with a hero in a novel enables us to realign
ourselves with ourselves. It is a kind of symbiotic
relationship. The reader gets into the work by taking

on the characteristics of the hero and the hero in
turn takes on the characteristics of the reader.
There is a mutual adaptation of perspectives. For
example, in Arthur Miller's play 'The Crucible', John
Proctor is presented as a plausible hero who manages
to maintain his personal integrity in spite of im-
mense physical and emotional pressures inflicted upon
him by his religious persecutors. Rather than confess that he is in league with the devil, he goes to
the gallows. To the extent that we are able to
identify with John Proctor's dilemma, we are able to
imaginatively enact his predicament and work out our
own personal response to his situation. We live
through the episode with John Proctor and he inspires
and fills us with the hope that perhaps we would be
able to respond to situations with like courage.
Identification with the work guarantees a form of existence which is not dependent upon generalized conceptions of man conferred on us mediately by others,
but gives significance to our personal style of existence by confirming our freedom to create preferred
versions of humanity.

We get pleasure in contemplating states of affairs
which reflect the significance we and others attach
to our lives. We saw that the pleasure or pain we derive from contemplating states of affairs or objects
depended upon the extent that they confirmed or dis-
confirmed those features in our life to which we
attach significance, and of which having personal
worth is the supreme example. However, in non-
artistic instances, the relation between some confirming states of affairs and the set of values in
terms of which we recognize this worth is contingent,
that is, typically, no internal identifying relationship exists between the distinctive patterning of the
activity or object and our nature. Whereas in the
work of art, we attach significance to its features
precisely because it reflects our distinctiveness.
The nature of the connection between the ordinary
perceptual objects and the spectator then is external.
For example, in the case of holiday souvenirs, the
source of value is externally related to the concrete
objects. It reminds the viewer of an enjoyable episode in his life. The particular nature of the
holiday-as-enjoyed doesn't inhere in the distinctive

patterning of the object's surface. Practically, any
object associated with the holiday would do, and the
same object would serve a similar purpose for other
holiday makers. It relates to the spectator's experience in a wholly generalized way. Whereas the
point of art is to embody the distinctive experience
of the artist in the making: 'the affirmation of the
inwardness of subjectivity' (Marcuse, p.4, 1979).
One can imagine a poet, for example, composing a work
depicting the particularity of the episode, if successful the patterning of the work would depict the
event as thus depictable in this medium i.e. there
would be an internal identifying relationship between
the elements constituting the poem and the event as
thus depicted.

The subjective response to the 'subjective' in a work
of art is important because it marks off the aesthetic
from those activities which confer worth on someone
because they conform to a standard of general
approval which anyone achieving the appropriate
standard would deserve. For example, in Mathematics
and Science our personal competence is dependent upon
conforming to public standards. The ability to do
quadratic equations confers a personal sense of worth
only if we accept the public evaluations of merit.
Whereas art confers personal worth because it exhibits to the maker the significance of his individual
marks in a medium i.e. individual marks which register his potentiality to transcend his mundane purposes. There is an obvious sense in which noticing
the aspect of something in itself confers significance on it, i.e. we register its existence by pick-
ing it out from a range of other features. For example, if as individuals we were completely similar
in all respects it would not only be impossible for
others to notice us, but it would also be impossible
for us to notice ourselves. To take another example,
when we take a tin of Heinz chicken soup off the
shelf of a supermarket, everything else being equal,
we don't need to notice anything about that particular tin apart from the fact that it falls under a
general description which any other of the tins on
the shelf would fit. At base, the distinctiveness of
our physical features (e.g. red hair) make us con-
spicuous to others, and therefore to ourselves.

However, a distinctive feature of being human is having and being able to formulate purposes, and physical characteristics are noticed as distinguishing
features just so long as they relate to these purposes. If our being is constituted in the noticing
then those features which are noticed constitute our
being. Insofar as we conform to descriptions applicable to any person (e.g. father, customer, priest) we
exist, but in a wholly generalizable way. The arts,
on the other hand, give distinctiveness to our individual perspective. In making a work of art the artist exhibits his freedom to formulate purposes by intentionally choosing the elements in his work. The
artist notices 'these aspects rather than those' and
we recognize his intention that we should notice
'these aspects rather than any others'. However,
there is no instrumental reason why we should find
these marks more significant than any others. That
is, they are not a means to some end whose significance is not immediately assessable in the making, in
the way, for example, the formulation of marks on a
map may lead me to my desired destination. The formulation of the marks have a point in relationship to
a pre-established end. And if I don't attach significance to the features of a work of art, then in
more than a tautological sense they don't have significance (for me). For it is of little satisfaction
to the spectator that someone else finds the features
of a work significant. The fact that someone else
finds, for example, a painting significant may be a
reason for trying to appreciate it, but it is never a
reason for appreciating it. The value of a work of
art lies in the relationship between the perceiver's
individual perspective and the features embodied in
the painting. Existentially they are not detachable,
both depend on each other for their existence.

The up shot of what I am saying is that in creating
and appreciating works of art, they exhibit to us
that which we fundamentally value, namely, the freedom to attach significance to things for their own
sake. We give significance to ourselves in giving
significance, on appropriate grounds, to works of
art. Analogously, a person affirms his moral worth
in appropriate circumstances by asserting his rights,
and from his point of view if he isn't prepared to

assert his rights, he has no rights, although he may
come to recognize he has rights by the way other
people treat him. Correspondingly, the work of art
has no significance if the viewer doesn't give it
significance and consequently the viewer fails in
that context to register his worth. For ultimately
the significance of a work of art is dependent on the
viewer's capacity to value something for its own sake.
So my argument is that in appreciating and creating
works of art we reveal to ourselves a freedom: this
freedom manifests itself in the patterning of sensuous form. The importance of the sensuous consists
in the immediacy of the apprehension, and the patterning makes possible the fusing of meaning. The
artist creates an imaginative dimension which tran-
scends the practical reality of our everyday purposes. He reveals in his creations possible ways of
interpreting our existence, he shows the possibility
of transforming a way of life, and importantly he
shows what it is for someone to value something not
merely as a means to something else but for its own
sake. Even if this only approximates to the truth
then the relevance of art in the education of a child
is obvious. It is a mode of awareness which gives
significance to his individual perspectives and
brings him up against the perspectives of others.
Unlike other subjects, at least, in so far as they do
not approximate to the aesthetic, the arts enriches
his life by registering aspects of his being as meaningful, a criterion of which is pleasure he gets in
the looking. The kind of relevance that engagement
in the arts has is not to be characterized in terms
of its instrumentality to other desirable ends or to
its inherent qualities, but rather to the fact that
it is instrumental to valuing our subjective response
to the world. The aesthetic engagement confirms our
existence as free, creative and imaginative beings.
In so doing, it enables us to share the world and as-
pirations of other men. Each work reveals our freedom and this awareness charges us with hope in the
recognition of the permanent possibility of changing
the texture of our lives. Even the educational pragmatist would find it difficult to refute the relevance of these ends to children in school: one must
but hope he will accept the legitimacy of the argument that the arts contribute to these ends in a very

special way. We have a responsibility in respect of
all children whatever their position in life to provide them with experiences which on appropriate
grounds enhance their individual worth; and art is
such an experience.

REFERENCES

Bruner, Jerome S. (1971). The Relevance of Education.
    George Allen and Unwin.

Eisner, Elliot. (1972). Educating Artistic Vision.
    Collier Macmillan.

Kant, I. (1951), Critique of Judgement. Hafner
    Publishing Co.

Marcuse, Herbert. (1979). The Aesthetic Dimension.
    The MacMillan Press Ltd.

Ross, Malcolm. (1980). Hard Core: The Predicament of
    the Arts. (This volume.)

Satre, Jean-Paul. (1943). Being and Nothingness.
    Methuen & Co. Ltd.

Stokes, Adrian. (1963). Painting and the Inner
    World. Tavistock Publications.

Wollheim, Richard. (1979). The Sheep and the
    Ceremony. Cambridge University Press.

You are the Music

MALCOLM ROSS

"For most of us, there is only the
    unattended
 Moment, the moment in and out of time,
 The distraction fit, lost in a shaft
    of sunlight,
 The wild thyme unseen, or the winter
    lightning
 Or the waterfall, or music heard so
    deeply
 That it is not heard at all, but you
    are the music
 While the music lasts."

                    T.S. Eliot, Four Quartets.

In this paper I want to consider two rather difficult
questions: why the popular idea of arts education
places arts teachers beyond the educational palings,
and how that idea might be favourably modified, without seriously compromising the values that arts
teachers rightly cherish. It would clearly be helpful if arts educators were able, for instance, to
demonstrate that the various activities associated
with art were inherently both healthy and morally
committed! I believe we can make some modest claims
under both these heads.

Arthur J. Newman (1980) hypothesises a direct relation
between aesthetic development and moral development.
He takes Lawrence Kohlberg's (Lickona, 1976) account

AI - K

of the sixth (and highest) level of moral growth and
suggests a strong connection between the various at-
tributes ascribed to moral maturity and the factors
essential to the making of sensitive, aesthetic
judgments. (I shall be considering these factors in
detail a little later in this paper.)

Newman wishes to see moral education strengthened by
infusing the curriculum "with learning experiences
designed to enhance aesthetic sensitivity" - his
point being that there is an essentially aesthetic
dimension (he speaks of "nonrational, nonlinear and
nondiscursive cognitive processes") to moral judgment.
His point is not to equate the moral with the
aesthetic. Nor does he intend to repudiate rational
analytic mental processes as instrumental in bringing
about moral development, and, indeed, as part of the
machinery of moral judgment making. He sees the
aesthetic and the rational complementing each other
in mature moral responsiveness while at the same time
admitting that there might be no consistent behavioural transfer between purely aesthetic and non-
aesthetic contexts. He cautions -

> "The historical record reflects all too
> many instances of heinous applications
> of a finely tuned imagination."

Newman's prime concern in his paper is with the likely advantage for a child's moral development of a
school curriculum that pays attention to sensitizing
his or her aesthetic responses. He is insisting upon
the aesthetic dimension of moral intelligence and upon the need to foster and enhance it in the interests
of children's general moral education. Such a contention seems both plausible and sensible.

But what about the "aesthetic-moral relationship hypothesis" itself? This surely goes well beyond merely recognising that moral judgments are made, at
least in part, on the basis of essentially aesthetic-
type mental processes. There is an inference of
inter-relatedness between the moral and the aesthetic
domains: a proposition that, although moral and
aesthetic judgments might be deployed in respect of
different objects and in special situations, both

activate the same mental processes. And, although
transfer from one context to the other cannot be pre-
dicated, there is, nevertheless, some hope that in
certain circumstances maturity of response in the
aesthetic field might well reinforce, even if it did
not guarantee, mature moral behaviour.

The implication of this hypothesis for teachers of
the arts and aesthetics could be of the utmost significance. If the link could be established between
aesthetic education and the building of acceptable
value systems and the prompting of moral attitudes in
children arts teachers would have a very powerful
claim to legitimacy indeed. In a single bound it
would be possible to overlap the all-too-familiar and
now widely disparaged apparatus of authorization by
examination and appeal directly to undisputed, non-
contended human values. The arts would be legitimate
because they developed the love of truth, the feeling
for good form (ie. beauty), and the capacity for empathy. These objectives would be self-evidently
valuable as in any humane education. We should, at a
stroke, have done away with the proliferating of
cost-effective rationalizations of the outcomes of
arts education, and we would be able to insist with
quiet confidence that our work was civilising in the
best possible sense. That education in and through
the arts was education for goodly living as well as
for the good life.

A number of questions immediately suggest themselves.

1. Is the aesthetic intrinsically moral?

2. How legitimate would the claim for the aesthetic-
    moral hypothesis seem to artists and arts
    teachers? Is there any evidence that such a re-
    lationship is held to exist - amongst those
    directly concerned?

3. Could the link between the aesthetic and the moral
    be substantiated objectively? Could we show for
    instance that the empathy developed in and through
    aesthetic encounters might reveal itself as a
    general attribute of an individual's personality
    available (even if not always deployed) across

the whole range of experience?

4. Given this commitment to developing a morally
    valuable cluster of responses would it not still
    be necessary to devise some means of assessing
    the acquisition and incidence of these desired
    competences? Would we not wish to know whether
    the outcomes of aesthetic education were indeed
    what was intended? Or must such outcomes neces-
    sarily be taken on trust - as a matter of faith
    as it were?

5. Given such an emphasis what would be the appro-
    priate conditions and what would be the content
    for a curriculum devised to develop children's
    aesthetic sensitivity?

In the course of this paper I shall only be able to
touch on some of these issues. My principal purpose
is to propose a particular - not, I'm sure, a new -
emphasis for arts education, one which, hopefully,
would lend greater authority to our work as arts
teachers and, at the same time, give our work a more
popular appeal.

It is usual these days to see the arts subjects with
their backs to the curriculum wall: my own paper on
the Core Curriculum, written to provide a take-off
point for this Conference, assumes this attitude.
And I don't deny that our response to the pressures
upon us has to be both positive and strenuous - there
can be no doubt of that. By some means the future of
the arts at the centre of children's education has to
be assured and there does seem some danger that that
assurance might be in question.

One powerful way of alleviating our difficulties
would, I suggest, be to help those "outside" arts
education - politicians, parents, headteachers,
directors of education - to perceive the arts differently. If they were able to do so they might feel
differently about them and be less likely to fall
prey to the kinds of argument now being deployed
against the arts, arguments raised upon grounds of
practical utility and economic effectiveness, both
wholly inappropriate to any sympathetic understanding

of the nature and function of art. However, before
we can provide a persuasively attractive image of the
arts for the non-arts world we have to find one that
arts people themselves can own up to and feel com-
plete commitment for. How realistic such a project
would be must, I suppose, remain something of an open
question.

I have for a long while argued that arts teachers
could make common cause and this series of annual
conferences takes as its point of departure the notion that the arts subjects constitute a single discipline, a unique way of knowing, within the curriculum. However, experience suggests that reaching an
acceptable consensus is a far from easy task. Arts
teachers are divided not only by their own specialisms
as discrete art forms but, perhaps more significantly,
(and more deeply) along ideological lines - a notion
developed in several other papers in this volume. In
seeking a formula for bringing the arts together as a
single force in education we are looking for an
ideology we can all share. I believe such an ideology
to be available, provided we can bear in mind that
our concern is, first and formost, with the educational role of the arts in the experience of all
children and not with the nature of art itself. I
want to formulate the aim of arts education as the
development of children's aesthetic sensitivity -
their aesthetic intelligence.

****

I have spoken of the need to change the image of arts
education. Before developing my alternative I should
perhaps spend a moment or two reviewing the stereotype as it exists at the moment. The "profile" I am
about to sketch is based on no statistical testing,
though it does derive in part from the survey conduct-
ed for the Schools Council (Ross, 1975): readers must
judge its accuracy against their own experience. What
I am suggesting is that the popular idea or image of
arts education does absolutely nothing to secure the
authorization of the arts within the curriculum and
that we must change the way people see the arts - in
particular the way they see arts education - if we

are to change the way they feel about them. The good
sense of this assessment is widely endorsed: the
critical question, however, concerns the nature of
any alternative image.

Much effort in recent years has gone into creating a
more legitimate image for the arts by attempting to
make them more or less indistinguishable from the
rest of the curriculum. That is to say, into showing
how like the rational, linear and discursive core of
the school curriculum the arts can be made to appear.
The emphasis upon Design Education is one instance of
this tendency - this seeking after a more legitimate
image. The drive to make the arts more readily examinable is another. I would argue that such moves
have by and large failed in their objective - not
least because they have alienated a good many arts
teachers and their pupils. Because the move is interpreted as a kind of 'selling out'. Furthermore,
and ironically, the hoped for legitimacy that was
thought to follow from more examinations in the arts
has proved a dead duck because no-one seems to feel
that, for instance, to have an 'A' level in drama
qualifies anyone for anything at all. Not even for
the study of drama in higher education. Such moves
have not changed the image of arts education for the
better.

It would, I suggest, make better sense to seek to
demonstrate rather the unique character of aesthetic
experience and to help people to see how the aesthetic
intelligence operates, in a special way, as a dimension of all intelligent behaviour. But I am rather
running ahead of myself.

I said I would attempt a profile of arts education
that would represent the popular view and account at
least in part for both our continuing low status in
education and the success, such as it is, of the current pressure against the arts. I would argue that
in a work-oriented, sexist society such as ours, the
arts in education suffer primarily because their
image is, essentially, illegitimate.

The two columns below represent a set of polarities
that determine the legitimacy of pursuits in schools.

(They are not without their application in the wider
context of social interactions outside the school.)
The factors in the left-hand column are legitimate
and valuable in terms of the dominant work/masculine
ethos of schooling. They are acceptable "clocks on"
criteria for action. Those in the right-hand column
belong to the illegitimate play/female category of
activities. A cursory reading of the D.E.S. paper
"A Framework for the Curriculum" (1980) identifies
the proposed core of subjects firmly by the left-hand
set of criteria, with all those aspects of the curriculum governed by the right-hand set out in the cold.
They are distinctly "clocks off" activities - not
time-free but time-bound by a different ordinance.
Time allowably "wasted" - for purposes of recreation
rather than creation. (The list is not intended to
be exhaustive.)

Work/Masculine	Play/Feminine
(Clocks on)	(Clocks off)
Interpretations	Mysteries
Logic	Imagination
Making	Tending/attending
Objective/public	Personal/private
Useful	Pleasurable
Reason	Intuition
Materialist	Transcendental
Ideas	Feelings
Productive skills	Unproductive skills
Predictable/accountable	Unpredictable/unaccountable
Regulated	Spontaneous

The arts subjects, I believe, are discounted in
schools because they conform to the illegitimate
play/female category. Nothing that anyone has been
able to do has given the lie to this evaluation and
all arts activities, like all leisure activities and
all women, suffer from type-casting when comparison
with the legitimate type is invoked. The whole climate of the current political, economic and educational crisis favours the traditional evaluation. It
follows that as long as the arts are perceived as
"clocks off" in a "clocks on" world they will continue
to have a bad time.

I have not discussed the personal image of the artist
because I'm less certain of its influence upon public
opinion. I think people at large probably still regard artists (painters and poets especially, musicians
and novelists less so) as odd-ball, and everyone
knows Van Gogh was miserable and went mad. But we
are more tolerant of certain deformities and non-
conformities than we used to be and few people,
probably, regard the person of the artist, despite
the eccentricities, with anything but bemused benign-
ity. It is not so much that artists, or arts teachers
for that matter, are illegitimate as persons: it is,
rather, that their livelihood is illegitimately made
and consequently felt to be non-serious and irrelevant
to the real business of life. Given such a swingeing
dismissal it is, perhaps, little wonder if artists
and arts teachers are tempted to shift their ground
and seek legitimacy on the other side of the fence.

It is, of course, being argued that far from wishing
to repudiate our stereotype as play/female we should
be capitalising on it for all we are worth. The
micro-chip revolution spells the end of work as the
western world has for centuries known it. We are
moving into the age of extended leisure for all and
of paid community action ("tending") as an alternative to paid manufacturing. The arts, we are told,
are headed for boom-time. What else are people going
to do? Arts education will on the one hand provide
the skills for a fruitful life and enforced recreation, and on the other hand create the mental attitudes necessary to allow people to adapt to new and
perhaps disturbing circumstances. I would not wish
to opt out of any opportunities that present themselves for making the arts signify in children's
lives in school and in their future lives as adults
and parents in the society of the future. However, I
would maintain there is nothing inherently new in all
this for us as arts teachers - and I have my own sus-
picions that the line dividing 'legitimate' work from
'illegitimate' play could easily become sharper
rather than more defuse. We may well see the emerg-
ence in time of a dominant social elite - harder and
more inscruitable than anything we know now. And the
arts would, in such circumstances, merely assume the
former role of religion: as the opium of the people.

The betrayal of the arts would thereby have been completed.

Our dilemma is to remain faithful to the traditional
role of the arts as personally and socially regener-
ative while repudiating the disqualifications of
illegitimacy: to claim the uniqueness of aesthetic
experience while demonstrating its ubiquity. I am
sure arts educators have been right, recently, to
concentrate on clarifying their understanding of
aesthetic experience itself - of the development of
the aesthetic intelligence as the basis of aesthetic
education. I think we may be approaching the time
when we can make our claim to a central position in
education stick and when we can begin to see a way of
improving our image without either lying down under
the old stereotyping or deserting the aesthetic for a
spurious legitimacy on altogether alien terms.

I think there might be something for arts education
in Newman's aesthetic-moral hypothesis. Not that our
case would be that you can approach moral education
through the arts - as you can approach history, geography, maths and whatever else through projects in
music, drama and painting. This particular curricular
stratagem is, of course, already well-tried, and not
without both appeal and success. There is an important issue to clear up here before I can come to my
main point: the distinction that must be drawn between using the arts as _instrumental_ to learning in
non-arts areas, and the arts as a way of knowing the
world in their own right. It is the distinction between art as illustration and art as icon or symbol.
However one understands the notion of art as symbol
there is general agreement that artistic images embody
meaning - that is to say, that they are non-
referential. In apprehending the sensuous form of
the art image we apprehend it as - in Louis Arnaud
Reid's terms - "meaning embodied". The images of art
work on us directly, and in their own way. They do
not depend for their aesthetic significance on their
relationship with some event, object, proposition or
idea outside themselves. Art used as illustration or
exemplification, art used instrumentally, whatever
its intrinsic aesthetic appeal, depends, for its ultimate legitimation, upon some extrinsic order of

things. The relevance of King Lear to a child's perception of the tragic potential latent in intimate
family relationships lies not in providing material
(documentation) for sociological or psychological analysis but in offering imaginative structures to re-
lease and articulate feelings. Art is a way of knowing, operating in accordance with its own laws: directly engaging the imagination to give form to feeling. As I have said, it can be used instrumentally.
But to be forced into a servicing role exclusively is
to emasculate art.

To return to my argument - or rather to Newman's. The
proposed aesthetic moral hook-up sees the aesthetic
not as instrumental to the process of moral development but as an essential dimension of the moral. It
is not simply that the arts can be seen to have moral
application - as they can have social or political
and religious application. It is to propose that the
arts are essentially moral, essentially spiritual as
forms of action and in terms of their attributed significance. That whatever other purposes they serve -
either in the lives of those who make art or of those
for whom art is made - the arts spring from the human
desire to create and cherish the beautiful.

Now I am aware that this assertion begs a number of
questions, not least what is here meant by 'beautiful'.
I shall hope to throw at least some light upon what I
mean. But the assertion must stand - and, if it is
to carry weight in the present education debate, its
appeal should be immediate and need no further apology.
I personally want to drop, at least for the time being,
arguments that make use of suspect words like
'expression' and 'feeling' and esoteric jargon terms
like 'sensate ordering' and 'subject-reflexive action'.
Such language may have its place in the theoretical
literature but what we are talking about here is the
public face of arts education and we need words and
ideas that everyone might use and feel at home with.
We are talking about the appeal we have to make that
goes at once from the heart of the aesthetic to the
hearts of ordinary men and women. We have essentially
to tell them what they already know and not mount a
painfully worked out technical argument that no-one
wants to bother with. Tell them what they know - but

have, perhaps, forgotten, or not thought worth remembering.

We have been looking at stereotypes - and have located
arts education in the soft, 'clocks off' realm of
things playful and feminine. I have suggested that
few people object strongly to the notion of the artist as a person. I want to say that there are positive features of what one might call the popular
image of art that are at least as well established as
any of the more desparaging stereoptypes: features
that Newman itemises in his paper as constituting the
aesthetic response. The point he makes is this:
there are features of aesthetic perceiving which in-
cline one to believe "that the process is - on some
occasions at least - intrinsically moral". I take
this to mean that the experience of art is an experience of values and of valuing, of moral perception.
I would want to say that the experiences of art are
essentially experiences of love: the intelligence of
love in action for which the Greeks use the work
agape: the tender-heartedness spoken of in St. Paul's
letter to the Corinthians as the greatest of the vir-
tues. Again I must appeal to the readers patience
until I can deal more fully with this assertion. The
assertion, to be quite clear, is that aesthetic experience - and hence aesthetic education - is centered
upon our capacity to act and perceive with love:
love of life, of living, of lives - our own and the
lives of others known and unknown to us.

The features of the aesthetic response singled out by
Newman as "intrinsically moral" are worth dwelling
upon. The first factor is what he calls "the necessarily non-stereotypic quality" of aesthetic knowing.
He quotes Iredell Jenkins (1958).

> "When our attitude toward things is pri-
> marily aesthetic it is the self-assertion
> of things of their own individual exist-
> ence and autonomy that dominates the
> experiential situation"

- a view that will be thoroughly familiar to everyone
with some knowledge of the literature of aesthetics.
It is frequently emphasized that the first feature of

aesthetic intentionality is a commitment to reverence
and savour experience for its own sake, for its intrinsic interest and irrespective of any extrinsic
application. Artistic vision is concerned with the
unique quality of the particular, with whatever constitutes the character, identity or presence of individuality. The essential and necessary form, the
comeliness, the truth of an object, a place, a person.
This is what I take Keats to mean when he says that
"Truth is beauty" and it is certainly the key to understanding the notion of the beautiful in the context of arts education. (The Greek for beauty is
EUMORPHIA: literally, 'good form'.) Aesthetic perception involves the capacity to respond to the
uniqueness, the singular quality of things - to value
individual integrity and to reject the cliche and the
stereotype. Another way of putting it would be to
say that aesthetic perception sees with the eye of
the child: or perhaps we need, rather, Abraham Maslow's
notion of second (ie. recovered) naivetee. Such
seeing is not merely believing, it is loving. In
this connection I warmly recommend two of
Whitman's poems (both impossible to quote from):
"Carol of Occupations" and "I Sing the Body Electric".

The second of Newman's "inviolable cannons" of the
aesthetic is the commitment to genuineness, to authenticity. There must be no dishonesty, no dissembling,
no affectation or mere conformity where aesthetic ex-
experience is concerned. Artistic illusion is
"allowed"; the true artist does not practice decep-
tion however. Aesthetic judgment is intensely sensitive to the notion of integrity, to things being
what they claim, seem or purport to be. Which is,
presumably, one of the reasons why so much heat is
generated over issues such as art forgery, copying,
"restoration" and the like. Such trustworthiness is
essential to any act of love.

Aesthetic perception respects individual identity and
demands integrity and honesty. It is further
characterised by a propensity for openness, a readiness to entertain a wide range of possibilities, so
sustain ambiguities and operate multi-dimensionally.
To postpone cognitive closure. This is, of course, a
well-known feature of creative thought generally and

betokens a personality capable of tolerating relatively high levels of uncertainty, suspense and even
frustration. Its positive pay-offs include the capacity to wait for novel perceptions and insights to
form - and the protection afforded against settling
for inappropriate or merely predictable solutions.
Multi-dimensionality as a frame (or framing) of mind
also permits healthy detachment, objectivity,
and humour to play their parts in the cognitive process. It saves healthy self-love from turning nar-
cissistic.

Newman's fourth criterion is the concept of "fittingness".

> "In the words of R.M. Ogden, 'a
> disposition to feel the completeness
> of an experience or event as being
> right and fit constitutes what we have
> called the aesthetic factor in per-
> ception'. This notion is akin to the
> classical Greek insistence that a pre-
> requisite for living the good life is
> personal mastery of appropriate form".

Fittingness is what I would call 'the feeling for
good form'; our sense of what Michael Tippett (1974)
has called "the comely and the beautiful - the seem-
liness or quality of things". It involves the capacity to judge things as wholes, to take all aspects
of the aesthetic object into account: holistic perception.

In this context I am reminded of another paper I was
reading recently written by René Welleck (1960) and
to be found in Thomas Sebeok's "Style in Language".
He is describing what I take to be the process of
aesthetic knowing. He calls it "the circle of understanding".

> "In reading with a sense for continuity,
> for contextual coherence, for wholeness,
> there comes a moment when we feel that
> we have 'understood', that we have
> seized on the right interpretation, the
> real meaning. The psychologists might

> say that this is a mere hunch, mere
> intuition. But it is the main source
> of knowledge in all humanistic branches
> of learning, from theology to juris-
> prudence, from philology to the history
> of literature. It is a process that
> has been called 'the circle of under-
> standing'. It proceeds from attention
> to a detail to an anticipation of the
> whole and back again to an interpreta-
> tion of the detail. It is a circle
> that is not a vicious but a fruitful
> circle. It has been defended and des-
> cribed by the great theorists of
> hermeneutics."

I have previously suggested a particular interpretation of the concept of beauty: I now want to modify
it and suggest that this sense of what is fitting
must also temper our perception and judgment of what
is beautiful. Indeed it occurs to me that in as much
as the aesthetic is concerned with discerning and
cherishing the beautiful all Newman's factors must to
some degree modify our understanding and use of that
term.

Finally Newman moves to the emotional and imaginative
dimension of aesthetic perception. He calls his last
feature, empathy. He writes

> "According to some, the aesthetic appre-
> hension of non human phenomena occurs
> as an interactive process of projecting
> the self into the object of perception
> while simultaneously introjecting the
> object into the self. Through an
> exercise of the imagination, the self-
> object distinction becomes obliterated;
> a unitary, inviolable whole is
> experienced."

I am reminded of the kind of things Stanley Spencer
was in the habit of saying about his own visionary
powers. Here he is in the recent Arts Council film
about his life and work describing a particular experience of painting.

"There was this kind of religious significance in life there, and a kind of
longing to be joined with and one with
that wonderful religious atmosphere, to
be sharing in it. Rather amazing in a
way. I think possibly that what was
happening was this: that with the
difference of a place there was also a
kind of forming of the different parts
of my own makeup.

I went over to the farm where our
cousins were and one of these cousins
used to say to me - Stanley, would you
like to come down Mill Lane with me?
I am just going to feed the calf. And
that was a joy to me. Amy would get
the bucket of milk and she would put
her hand down into the bucket - she
was weaning it. Now when I just thought
of that, not when I was looking at it
but when I got home, I thought: yes,
this is more it. I think you can see
how this design and composition is beginning to come into a thing, perform
this operation that I am praying and
hoping to be performed. The line of
the back of the calf slopes downwards
towards the bucket and the back of the
girl who is feeding the calf slopes
down towards the bucket also. That
seemed to have something of me realized.
I mean this internal feeling that I am
part of this wonder and secured in it.
It's like if you went to a lovely house
and said let me live here for always.
Well the design enables you to live in
that place always and forever more."

We are clearly here talking about the reciprocal interaction between maker and medium, audience and art-
efact, that I have already written about at length
(Ross, 1978). I want to go further now and say that
it is inherently just this capacity for imaginative
empathy, for feeling lovingly or tenderly towards the
phenomena of experience (including ourselves as

phenomena) that provides the possibility of aesthetic
perception. Whether we know it, recognise it as such
or not, acts of aesthetic perception are in this
sense acts of love. Such loving action is facilitated
by the engagement of the imagination which alone creates the vital bond between subject and object and
yields the kind of cosmic expansion of consciousness
which so many artists (and psychologists) have written
about. I recall the Eliot quotation which I used at
the beginning of this paper.

"You are the music while the music lasts."

Newman's five factors of aesthetic perception are, as
I have already said, familiar enough. His analysis
of the literature has allowed him I think to pick out
all the essential elements of the aesthetic response
though it was not, of course, part of his intention
in writing his paper to provide an exhaustive or detailed account of the aesthetic. He set out rather
to draw a parallel between features of aesthetic response and of mature moral behaviour. His point is
that the criteria that operate to distinguish
aesthetic knowing - an eye for the particular, a feeling for authenticity, the capacity for openness, a
sense of what is fitting and above all the capacity
for empathy - are all features of Kohlberg's sixth (and
ultimate) phase of moral development. Aesthetic
action is, in this sense therefore, moral action.
Although he draws back from asserting categorically
that the aesthetically mature person is also likely
to act in a morally mature way he nevertheless implies
that such a connection might not be impossible to
sustain. I would guess that there must be many people
who would agree that to be capable of acting imaginatively, of responding empathetically, of having a
feeling for quality, a sense of what is fit, of being
non-dogmatic, of entertaining alternatives and being
prepared to wait for the issues to clear, that these
qualities, while not ensuring good actions on all
occasions, nonetheless make good actions generally
more likely. I suggest that these qualitites are
self-evidently valuable and universally prized. That
all of us familiar with and committed to the arts
recognize them as inherent to the processes of artistic making and appreciation. Indeed, that they account

in large measure for much of our sense of the value,
the significance, the import of art.

So much that is written about aesthetics and art
seems to ignore this feeling that the arts count su-
premely in our experience: that they deal us experiences that equal in significance all our more
immediate encounters with life's great mysteries,
sorrows and joys. Herbert Marcuse, in his recent
book The Aesthetic Dimension (1979) certainly does
not shy away from this sense of the superordinate
value of art.

> "I shall submit the following thesis:
> the radical qualities of art, that is
> to say, its inditement of the estab-
> lished reality and its invocation of
> the beautiful image (Schoner Schein)
> of liberation, are grounded precisely
> in the dimensions where art transcends
> its social determination and emanci-
> pates itself from the given universe
> of discourse and behaviour while pre-
> serving its overwhelming presence.
> Thereby art creates the realm in which
> the subversion of experience proper to
> art becomes possible: the world formed
> by art is recognized as a reality
> which is suppressed and distorted in
> the given reality. This experience
> culminates in extreme situations (of
> love and death, guilt and failure, but
> also joy, happiness and fulfilment)
> which explode the given reality in the
> name of a truth normally denied or
> even unheard. The inner logic of the
> work of art terminates in the emergence
> of another reason, another sensibility,
> which defy the rationality and sensibil-
> ity incorporated in the dominant social
> institutions."

For Marcuse the whole point of art is indeed the
building of a truer, more beautiful world, one that
comes "closer to the heart's desire".

I am suggesting that these are the qualities in
children's responses that we, as arts teachers, are
seeking to develop. These are the qualities that define the aesthetic response. My contention is that
these qualities of human being are inherently and
self-evidently valuable. We might go further and
tentatively suggest that there could well be a connection between aesthetic sensitivity and honest and
loving dealings in the world: that the empathy, the
capacity for loving the otherness in people, places
and things, will colour the whole of a child's perceptions and infuse all his or her relationships.
It's hard to believe that, at least to some degree,
this might not be so - even if it is not going to be
easy to prove. The five factors of aesthetic perception constitute an alternative temporal dimension
to the "clocks on", "clocks off" continuum in education. It is in fact the aesthetic dimension of time
suspended, it is Eliot's "unattended moment" when
"all is always now". Art is one answer to man's
"immortal longings", and it is to the child's
"intimations of immortality" that our arts lessons
must minister.

In insisting that the features of the aesthetic response are self-evidently valuable I am not suggesting either that we now have our case for arts education sewn up or that we are somehow, excused accountability. I said earlier that we have to tell people,
in the first place, what they know. That means we
have to help them identify these qualities of human
being with their own aesthetic experience: and that
does require further thought. Not least because
people might need persuading that they have actually
had and, indeed, continue to have aesthetic experiences. I am saying that we have to deal with widespread general ignorance about the nature of
aesthetic experience and people's prejudice that such
experiences are reserved for a relatively small group
of "arts people" - professional artists and the well-
to-do patrons of the high arts - the custodians of
the finer feelings. It means demonstrating that ordinary men and women exercise aesthetic judgment, operate the criteria of originality, integrity, creativity, quality in their day to day decisions as
workers, home-makers, cooks, family tenders, church-

goers, counsellors, bingo players, gardeners, car
drivers, fun lovers. They may not always feel they
make the "right" decisions; they would probably admit
to ignorance and lack of judgment. But they would, I
feel sure, acknowledge the inherent value in being
able to see with the discerning eye of the expert, in
being able to tell the real from the phoney, in being
confident enough to try something new, to know a good
thing when you see it. Above all in being awake
enough (aesthetic enough) not to be conned. And
kind - or kindred heartedness - surely needs no
recommendation to anyone.

Asked to examine their own everyday experience - and
to forget their stereotyped notions of art and
artistic goings on - ordinary people would soon sense
the relevance of these things. They would wish, I
feel certain, to have their children educated in
these things. They will see what they already know,
and the case for aesthetic education, if not for arts
education, would be in the making at the very least.
And, be sure such an approach is in no sense a sell-
out, if you believe, as I do, that the aesthetic runs
through every aspect of life, is indeed an essential
dimension of consciousness itself and an invariant
feature of all intelligent action. Whether such decisions and judgments are actually "moral" or not may
be beside the point: which is that the aesthetic
sense is a vital faculty operating to bring us into
intimate association with every aspect of our trans-
actions with and in the world. It operates to guide
our judgments wherever considerations of quality, integrity, truthfulness and loving-kindness are oper-
ative and arts teachers must promote their work, in
the first place by pointing to the "aesthetic" activities of ordinary people in ordinary situations.

It might be felt in some quarters that I have sought,
unfairly, to play down the notion of art with a cap-
ital A in the interests of identifying a more acceptable image for arts education based on the idea of
aesthetic intelligence. That in giving prominence to
the concept of aesthetic sensitivity I have side-
stepped important problems concerned directly with
the nature and educational significance of work in
and works of art. Finding a suitable formula for

relating the two concepts art and aesthetics has
given me a good deal of trouble - which is why I was
initially grateful for the straightforward distinction proposed by Monroe C. Beardsley (1975) in his
paper "Semiotic Aesthetics and Aesthetic Education"
published in the Journal of Aesthetic Education.

> "The core, or central, or minimal
> artistic enterprise consists in a per-
> son's bringing into being an object or
> event with the idea of offering it, to
> others or himself, for aesthetic appre-
> hension .... This core concept analy-
> ses at once into two complimentary
> activities, which are conveniently re-
> ferred to as 'artistic' and 'aesthetic'.
> (1) There is a making or creating ....
> (2) There is apprehension of the work
> made."

The simplicity of this account lends it immediate
appeal, and there is clearly a sense in which it
represents the common-sense view of the two concepts.
Furthermore it serves to explain why creative arts
education has come to be identified with the making
of art and why we think of aesthetic education as
being predominantly concerned with art appreciation.
I don't wish now wholly to reject the formulation
though I do think it does need qualifying in important ways. The idea that works of art be defined as
phenomena realized for the purpose of aesthetic
apprehension seems fine as far as it goes. It distinguishes art from non-art in terms of the maker's
intentionality. Anything presumably may be apprehended aesthetically: it's just that works of art
were made to be so apprehended. Were made to satisfy
or gratify an appetite for aesthetic apprehension.

Using Maslow's well-known model we could conceive of
aesthetic action on two levels: as a feature of what
he calls Deficiency Need gratification, and, manifested in art, as a form of Being Need behaviour.
Which leads me to the first of my qualifications:
that a work of art is brought into being not simply
to provide an occasion for aesthetic apprehension but
actually to enhance or develop the apparatus of

aesthetic apprehension itself - the intelligence of
feeling so called. The making (and apprehension) of
works of art not only exercises but <u>educates the</u>
<u>aesthetic response</u>, essentially, as Louis Arnaud Reid
(1969) proposes, by creating new feeling experiences.
Here he is in close agreement with Richard Wollheim
(1979) who insists that all significant apprehensions
of works of art are acts of self-knowing. All of
which brings me to the point I want to make about arts
education as a feature of aesthetic education: the
arts are important because their principal purpose is
<u>the development of our aesthetic faculties</u>, the en-
hancement of feeling intelligence. If we want to exercise, refresh and develop our aesthetic perceptions
then we cannot do better than to make, perform and
respond to art. Which surely places the arts at the
centre of the aesthetic curriculum. I see arts
teachers as committed, first and foremost, to
<u>aesthetic education through the arts</u>.

My other qualification of the Monroe Beardsley doctrine concerns his apparently rather narrow, art-
based account of the aesthetic. It follows, I hope,
from what I have already said, that I want to claim a
much wider territory for aesthetic education - and
would see aesthetic judgments as influencing actions
in the world and not merely confined to a contempla-
tive, evaluatory role with particular respect to art.

The distinction between the aesthetic and the artistic can I think be further emphasised if we consider
the function of what have been called 'the aesthetic
emotions'. Essentially the aesthetic emotions are
those emotions we experience in acts of aesthetic
apprehension. Which means, necessarily, those
emotions that we experience in our search for originality, integrity, multi-dimensionality, fittingness
and identification (harmony or consonance between the
self and the other, the I and the thou). These
emotions include joy, sublimity, compassion, clarifi-
cation, cosmic union, delight, voluptuousness,
tenderness - to name only some. The arts are traditionally thought of as having to do with feeling:
I suggest that it is the business of art to give form
to feeling indeed <u>to create fictions that are feeling</u>
<u>forms</u>. (For Aristotle, art was essentially

'imitation'.) Our aesthetic emotions are evoked in
direct response to the imaginative act of fiction-
forming, to our perception of feeling, of experience,
taking or giving fitting form. Which accounts for
the sense we often have that works of art offer us a
feeling within an emotion - that we can take pleasure
in scenes apparently tragic and painful for instance.
Art is the essentially human face of the aesthetic.
In art man embodies aesthetic meaning, for himself
and for his fellow men. We turn to art for the
cleansing of the doors of our perceptions.

****

Perhaps I might, in conclusion, be permitted to try
to pull these somewhat random observations together
into a more measured statement concerning the nature
and scope of aesthetic education as I see it.

I accept the emphasis disclosed by the meaning of the
Greek root word <u>aesthesis</u> - literally 'sensation'.
Aesthetic experience is, essentially, an experience
of sensation: of sensory relationships or structures
- structures of sound, movement, light, heat, taste,
touch and so on. In some respects aesthetic education
begins and ends with cultivation of the child's powers
of sensory perception and control of those powers.
Time spent teaching children to use their senses with
relish as well as with discrimination is clearly an
important part of aesthetic education: good crafts-
manship, good physical co-ordination, an eye for
pleasing forms and a feeling for the inherent and intrinsic qualities of objects and events in the environment, are all valuable assets for young people
at work and in their homes.

Such an account of aesthetic education, unexceptionable
in itself, does not, however, do it full justice.
Sensory perception is certainly the basis of the
aesthetic: aesthetic perception however is a particular way of experiencing the world. I would suggest
a peculiarly human way. To understand what is special
about it we need to remind ourselves that, for the
infant, sensuous experiences are indistinguishable
from feelings, feelings of security and anxiety, of

love and anger, of confidence and helplessness. Sensation has, from the beginning of conscious life, a dual character: it is simultaneously a physical and a psychological experience. This dual character of sensuous experience is not lost as the child develops. Indeed it remains the essential feature of all aesthetic perception and accounts for our mature sense of beauty, our feelings for quality in objects, occasions and people, our response to art and appetite for the transcendental and the sublime. It is the prime function of the teacher of aesthetics, to use Blake's words, "to cleanse the doors of perception". To develop a child's potential and capacity for aesthetic absorbtion in phenomena as presences having meaning in-dwelling.

For the infant - and indeed through our life - aesthetic perception is a way of knowing. By which I mean that it is, in itself and without recourse to objective reasoning, a form of intelligence that allows us to make sense of the world. We sense the presence of people, objects and places directly and in an important sense know them, grasp their meaning immediately and intuitively. We become sensitive to the language of sensuous forms and we know both ourselves and the world in feeling: as adults we testify to the value of felt knowledge when we judge a situation as 'feeling right'. The infant knows its mother directly: her meaning is embodied in her form, a form sensuously grasped and understood. From that time on all sensuous phenomena are capable of making this double impact upon us, are the sensuous embodiments of meaning that is sensation imbued with feeling, value, character, presence, quality.

This is the special way of seeing, the seeing 'double', that we mean by aesthetic perception. Anything - art as well as non-art objects can be seen in this way. For the young child everything is seen this way. As he or she comes to distinguish between subjective and objective experience there develops the capacity to switch channels and direct sensuous grasp tends to be replaced by reasoned abstraction as the principal mode of intelligence. "Seeing double" may actually become difficult unless the balance between this older mode and the new conceptual power is

preserved. It is never wholly lost - everyone at
some time or other displays a feeling for quality and
allows the feel of the thing to influence their judgment. But the "intelligence of feeling", as it has
been called, is notoriously misprized in our own
culture.

The artist, whatever his apparent motive in making
art, is driven first of all by the longing to form:
all his aesthetic creative acts are essentially acts
of love-in-the-making. The Greek word for artist is
kalitechne - a "good maker". One who cares for and
creates good forms or, to use another Greek word,
kalaesthesia, "good sensations". Beauty is a key
feature of aesthetic experience. We actively seek
not just forms but good forms. We are concerned not
simply with qualitites but with quality. And the
good forms of art, like all things well formed, are
somehow on the side of life: they are well adapted to
their function, economical of energy, intelligently
realized. They work as wholes. Literally they are
holy - worthy of our reverence and our cherishing.
The artist is committed to the idea of holy and
beautiful forming - his apparent subject matter may
be ugly, nevertheless it is redeemed by its embodiment
in harmonious form. Above all by its commitment to
vital truth, to the aesthetic zest for life.

Redeemed but not necessarily resolved: art carries us
beyond the bare facts into the world of vision and of
the transcendental, calling us continually to remake
our perceptions of the world, to break new ground.
Art offers us knowing, enlightenment, a passionate
challenge rather than consolation. Marcuse (1979)
has described art as "the struggle for the impossible
against the unconquerable, whose domain can perhaps
nevertheless be reduced". We make our memorials out
of our frailties - we assert our integrity out of our
vulnerability.

It is the business of art not only to feed our powers
of aesthetic perception but to restructure them - to
make us grow as aesthetic intelligences. Growing so
we become capable of increasingly complex and subtle
feeling responses, of coping with the affective con-
sequences of our encounters in the world. Through

acts of aesthetic judgment we discover how to give
shape to the world of feeling and how to act responsibly, imaginatively and above all with love in the
world. As I have always maintained, there is a sense
in which every man and every woman, every child is
and always has been a poet and an artist - aflame
with a divine fire, always capable of the vision that
Stanley Spencer maintained all his life and which
Thomas Traherne, the 17th century divine, lost with
childhood only to recover after an arduous struggle -

> "When I was a child my Knowledge was
> Divine. I knew by Intuition those
> things which since my Apostasie, I
> collected again, by Highest Reason ....
> The Corn was Orient and Immortal Wheat,
> which never should be reaped, nor was
> ever sown. I thought it had stood
> from Everlasting to Everlasting. The
> Dust and the Stones of the Street were
> as Precious as Gold. The Gates were
> at first the End of the World, the
> Green Trees when I saw them first
> through one of the Gates Transported
> and Ravished me; their Sweetness and
> unusual Beauty made my Heart to leap,
> and almost mad with Extasie, they were
> such Stand and Wonderful Things ....
> Boys and Girls Tumbling in the Street,
> and playing, were moving Jewels. I
> knew not that they were Born and should
> Die. But all things abided Eternaly as
> they were in their Proper Places.
> Eternity was Manifest in the Light of
> the Day, and some thing infinit Behind
> everything appeared; which talked with
> my Expectation and moved my Desire."

This is not, I hope, a kind of nostalgic crying after
a Never Never Land: I sense I am being anything but
sentimental. What I am proposing is a highly
disciplined, highly responsible, constantly challenging, constantly disturbing approach to the education
of what Giambattista Vico (1725) called "sapienza
poetica" - the poetic wisdom of Everyman.

References

Beardsley, Monroe C. (1975), Semiotic Aesthetics and Aesthetic Education, Journal of Aesthetic Education, Vol. 9, No. 3, July.

Jenkins, Iredell, (1958). Art and the Human Enterprise. Harvard U.P.

Kohlberg, Lawrence, in Lickona, Thomas (1976), Moral Development and Behaviour. Holt, Rinehart and Winston.

Marcuse, Herbert (1979), The Aesthetic Dimension. Macmillan.

Newman, Arthur J. (1980), Aesthetic Sensitizing and Moral Education. Journal of Aesthetic Education, Vol. 14, No. 2, April.

Reid, Louis Arnaud (1969), Meaning in the Arts. Allen and Unwin.

Ross, Malcolm (1975), Arts and the Adolescent. Evans Methuen.

Author Index

Subject Index

174